How to Guide

Recruiting Volunteers

Attracting the people you need

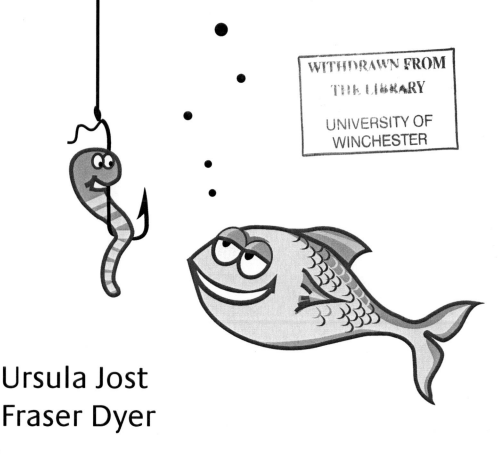

Ursula Jost
Fraser Dyer

DIRECTORY

Published by the Directory of Social Change (registered Charity no. 80051)

Head office: 24 Stephenson Way, London NW1 2DP

Northern office: Federation House, Hope Street, Liverpool L1 9BW
Tel: 08450 77 77 07

Visit www.dsc.org.uk to find out more about our books, subscription funding websites and training events. You can also sign up for e-newsletters so that you're always the first to hear about what's new.

The publisher welcomes suggestions and comments that will help to inform and improve future versions of this and all of our titles. Please give us your feedback by emailing publications@dsc.org.uk.

It should be understood that this publication is intended for guidance only and is not a substitute for professional or legal advice. No responsibility for loss occasioned as a result of any person acting or refraining from acting can be accepted by the authors or publisher.

First published 2002
Reprinted 2006, 2010 and 2013

ISBN 978 1 903991 20 6

British Library Cataloguing in Publication Data
A catalogue record for this book is available from the British Library

Cover design by Kate Bass
Original text design by Sarah Nicholson
Typeset by Marlinzo Services, Frome, Somerset
Printed and bound by CPI Group (UK) Ltd, Croydon CR0 4YY

CONTENTS

About the Directory of Social Change   iv

About the authors   v

Introduction   1

Chapter 1   Planning your volunteer recruitment   5

Chapter 2   Recruiting the skills you need   21

Chapter 3   Recruiting through your network   29

Chapter 4   Recruitment messages that get results   37

Chapter 5   Keep it up   47

Chapter 6   Making your organisation attractive to volunteers   55

Chapter 7   Diversifying your volunteers   63

Chapter 8   Use your imagination   75

Appendix 1   Who can volunteer with you?   93

Appendix 2   Sample EO policy statement for volunteers   96

Useful Addresses   97

Further Reading   105

ABOUT THE DIRECTORY OF SOCIAL CHANGE

DSC has a vision of an independent voluntary sector at the heart of social change. The activities of independent charities, voluntary organisations and community groups are fundamental to achieve social change. We exist to help these organisations and the people who support them to achieve their goals.

We do this by:

- providing practical tools that organisations and activists need, including online and printed publications, training courses, and conferences on a huge range of topics
- acting as a 'concerned citizen' in public policy debates, often on behalf of smaller charities, voluntary organisations and community groups
- leading campaigns and stimulating debate on key policy issues that affect those groups
- carrying out research and providing information to influence policymakers.

DSC is the leading provider of information and training for the voluntary sector and publishes an extensive range of guides and handbooks covering subjects such as fundraising, management, communication, finance and law. We have a range of subscription-based websites containing a wealth of information on funding from trusts, companies and government sources.

We run more than 300 training courses each year, including bespoke in-house training provided at the client's location. DSC conferences, many of which run on an annual basis, include the Charity Management Conference, the Charity Accountants' Conference and the Charity Law Conference. DSC's major annual event is Charityfair, which provides low-cost training on a wide variety of subjects.

For details of all our activities, and to order publications and book courses, go to www.dsc.org.uk, call 08450 777707 or email publications@dsc.org.uk

ABOUT THE AUTHORS

Fraser Dyer worked in the UK voluntary sector for twenty-seven years, where he previously managed volunteer programmes for Traidcraft and Greenpeace. From 1991 he was a management consultant and trainer, running hundreds of volunteer management workshops in Britain, Ireland and abroad–often alongside Ursula Jost with whom he was a partner in Spiral Associates for six years. He has also coached clients on work and leadership issues.

Fraser made a career change in 2009 when he was ordained as an Anglican priest. He is currently the incumbent of St. Anne and All Saints Church, South Lambeth which of course still involves him in work with volunteers.

Ursula Jost was a founding partner of Spiral Associates, which went on to become the UK's leading firm of training consultants specialising in volunteer management. Previously she was a business development manager and business analyst in the US and Switzerland, and has a master's degree in Industrial Administration. Ursula has been involved in the UK voluntary sector as consultant, trainer and volunteer since 1986. She was Chair and subsequently a Trustee of the Kensington and Chelsea Volunteer Bureau. She also served as President of the Swiss Church in London between 2000 and 2012.

INTRODUCTION

Britain has a tremendous tradition of volunteering. People from all walks of life give their time freely to help others in need, to campaign for a cause, to improve their community, or to offer mutual support to others who have the same passions or problems as themselves. Almost half the adult population in the UK does some form of voluntary activity, and in turn they take a part in the nation's second biggest leisure activity.

Volunteering is more than just a hobby, though. The work that volunteers do is essential to the functioning of our society. Volunteers deliver a significant proportion of community services – in schools, hospitals, family homes, community centres, forests, parks, museums, playing fields, theatres, animal sanctuaries and many other settings. We've come to rely heavily on them to sustain our social care provision, heritage, environment and the arts.

The work of volunteers extends beyond maintaining the status quo. They lobby for change, campaign against injustice, and speak up on behalf of the marginalised, oppressed and abused. They feed the hungry, visit the sick and imprisoned, comfort the bereaved, and befriend the lonely.

They also have fun. Whether running children's clubs, coaching sports activities, conserving the countryside or raising money by bathing in baked beans, the sound of laughter is never far from a group of volunteers.

If volunteers are important to us, the opportunity to volunteer is equally important to them. Many can testify to the way that voluntary work has given them more than just a jolly good time – lasting friendships, personal development, new skills, a route through depression or bereavement, a foothold on the jobs ladder, a means of giving something back to society, a sense of purpose, the satisfaction of having achieved a goal, and much, much more.

In the last twenty years we've seen some important changes to the way volunteers are utilised within the community. The range of roles that volunteers undertake seems to grow ever more diverse. Increasingly, volunteering has become recognised as relevant work experience, helping young people to get jobs and older people to change career paths. And the methods that organisations use to manage volunteers have become more organised, structured and professional.

What doesn't seem to have changed so much are the ways in which volunteers are recruited. Finding an adequate supply of people to run their services or assist their staff continues to be a struggle for many organisations. While demand for volunteers has grown, the strategies for finding them have stagnated. Recruitment ads are looking tired, generic and unimaginative.

This is not entirely the fault of volunteer recruiters. Many of those who are responsible for finding and managing volunteers are expected to perform too many other tasks and activities. Management committees, trustees and senior management need to wake up to the fact that volunteer involvement doesn't happen by magic. If the volunteer programme is going to run efficiently (and safely), then adequate time and resources need to be allocated to run it. This is unlikely to happen when responsibility for volunteers is tacked onto the end of another job.

Finding enough time to commit to recruitment is likely to be one of the biggest hurdles you face. Sadly, you will not find any short cuts within these pages. There are no instant solutions, or easy answers, for the key to successful recruitment lies in thorough strategic planning and regular ongoing activity. No matter how helpful or interesting you find this book, if you can't allocate sufficient time to recruitment you are unlikely to overcome the many challenges that finding volunteers presents.

We believe that success in recruiting volunteers is measured by finding *enough* of the *right* people for your organisation. In other words, you will not only recruit enough people, but they will also have the skills, commitment and qualities that are necessary to fulfil their role effectively. We have therefore written at length about being clear on who you want to recruit, and on strategies for successfully seeking out and attracting them to your organisation. We have not discussed selection and screening methods, or other issues related to volunteer management after the point of application.

One of the difficulties we've faced in writing about volunteers has been the diversity of organisations that involves them. We've tried to avoid making assumptions about the kind of organisation you belong to. You may, or may not, have employees. Perhaps you have clients or service-users, but maybe you don't. You could be politically or religiously motivated, or neither of those. You might be a small community project, or a large multi-million pound charity. Given all the variations in the volunteering world, it is inevitable that some of the examples or situations we describe, or terms we use, will be unfamiliar to you. While we've aimed to talk in general terms, we also wanted to give specific examples. You might find you need to translate some of the ideas and principles we share to make them appropriate to your organisation. For example, we regularly use the title 'volunteer coordinator' to describe the person who organises volunteer involvement and recruitment in your organisation. We realise that many projects won't have an employee with that job title but hope that you can equate that function with however you undertake it in your setting.

Over the years we have run workshops on volunteer recruitment for hundreds of people. We thought we knew something about the topic when we started out, but it was nothing compared to how much we learned from the experiences and insights of our course participants. A great many of the lessons in this book were learned from them and we'd like to say a big 'thank you' to them.

We are also grateful for the help, support and advice given to us during the writing of this book by the following people: John Bailey, Alison Baxter, Kate Bowgett, Rosemary Brown, Philip Carraro, Paul Chaplin, Eildon Dyer, Elizabeth Dyer, Anne Green, Nan Hawthorne, Elizabeth Heren, Rob Jackson, Gareth Jenkins, Nick King and Gerry Leighton, Shaun Levin, Bridget Morris, Mark Restall, John Stormont, Jamie Thomas, Margaret Thomas, Meena Varma and Stephanie Willats.

Fraser Dyer and Ursula Jost
April 2002

PLANNING YOUR VOLUNTEER RECRUITMENT

Why plan?

Have you ever set off on a trip without knowing where you are going? You just took off – perhaps with a friend, or the family – and followed your nose, without any idea of what your destination would be? For an afternoon out, or a day trip, it can be quite exciting to see where you end up.

But what about a holiday abroad? Would you do it then? Most people usually prefer to go on a planned holiday. They want to know beforehand where they are going, how they will reach their destination, and what they can expect in terms of climate, culture and comfort when they get there. Indeed many people don't even want to organise the trip themselves, and prefer to use a travel agent to arrange much of it.

Recruiting volunteers is similar to organising people to go on a journey. Before you set out you will need to do some planning and organising. Like travellers, most potential volunteers want to know what lies in store – the type of work they will be expected to do, at what times, the location, and whether any particular skills or qualities are required. It will also help if they know what people they will be working with, as well as how they will be prepared and supported in their work.

Some holidaymakers want to adapt their travel arrangements to suit their individual needs and interests. How flexible can you be in adapting to the individual needs and interests of your potential volunteers? Does everyone have to be a clone in the same tightly defined roles, or are you prepared to make volunteering with you attractive to a wide range of people by tailoring voluntary work to each person's requirements?

It is not only your new volunteers who want to know what lies ahead. Your existing volunteers, staff, trustees and others will want to know what implications arise for them as a result of your recruitment activity. By taking time to organise and plan your recruitment, you will help to prepare them for your new arrivals. Relevant service-users, staff, supporters or members may want to be consulted about the creation of new volunteering roles. In addition, staff need to be trained in how to manage and support volunteers effectively, and your trustees need to approve your volunteer policies.

Most importantly, perhaps, a well thought out plan will help you to be more effective and efficient in your recruitment efforts. In other words, planning leads to success.

The planning process

You need to be clear about the type of journey you are inviting volunteers to embark on, and have clear goals which define why you want to involve them, where, and at what cost. Your plan should also outline the best way to achieve these goals and whom you will need to involve. A plan of this sort will save you time, money and energy, and help to gain the goodwill and support of your colleagues.

As you may be beginning to realise, your plan for volunteer involvement needs to cover more than just how you are going to find people. The pieces need to be in place for the rest of your volunteer programme too. The chart opposite provides an overview of the areas that you will want to organise or review before beginning to recruit new volunteers.

In our work with voluntary organisations we've seen so many problems that were caused by a lack of planning:

- volunteers arriving for work and finding nothing to do because no one has defined their roles;
- resentment of volunteers among existing staff who have not been consulted, informed or trained about volunteer involvement;
- volunteers who get upset because their roles are suddenly changed;
- established volunteers who, out of suspicion or fear, fail to be welcoming towards newcomers;
- volunteers leaving because the work wasn't what they expected, or because it was badly organised;
- complaints from clients about the service from volunteers because no one has explained what a volunteer is (and isn't) permitted to do.

When volunteer coordinators struggle to recruit enough volunteers, or find themselves with a problematic volunteer programme on their hands, it is virtually always the result of poor planning. It may feel (and it is) very time consuming to put together a proper plan for the programme, but the mess resulting from a failure to plan can take much longer to sort out.

Recruiting new volunteers – planning overview

Planning and organising

- Establish goals and budget for overall volunteer programme
- Define roles for volunteers
- Develop volunteer policies
- Set up insurance and expenses payments for volunteers
- Prepare staff, clients and existing volunteers for new volunteers.

Recruitment

- Clarify recruitment goals and budget
- Identify appropriate recruitment methods and strategies.

Selecting volunteers

- Specify criteria for each voluntary role
- Choose appropriate selection methods
- Agree who is involved in selection process.

Inducting and training volunteers

- Design induction programme
- Conduct training needs analysis.

Supervising and supporting volunteers

- Agree how volunteers will be supported in their work
- Decide who needs to be involved in support and supervision.

An overall volunteer strategy

You can't plan recruitment without a strategy for the whole volunteer programme. When you go shopping for clothes you don't buy a shirt or a blouse simply because you like it. Even when you buy something on impulse, your mind considers a range of factors, such as can you afford it? Does it fit you? Will it match other clothes you already have? Is it suitable for work?

Before going out to find new volunteers you need to be sure that their involvement makes sense within the wider framework of your organisation, and your volunteer programme. Is your recruitment plan congruent with the overall strategy for the volunteer programme? How will new volunteers help your organisation fulfil its mission and purpose? What resources – including a budget – do you have at your disposal? Where do you most urgently need the help of volunteers, and where do you need their long-term support?

In a charity we shall call 'Blue,' there was no plan at all for the volunteer programme and no organised recruitment. As Blue had a high media profile, and worked in a field that had much popular support, they were fairly well off. A number of Blue's donors offered to come in and help out at the office to support the work of the staff team. Staff tended to call upon volunteers when they were stressed and had a mountain of paperwork stacking up on their desks, but they didn't take time to define the work that volunteers would do or to calculate the time it would take. Staff would often promise volunteers verbally that they would have an interesting and responsible workload, but it frequently amounted to little more than filing and photocopying. When volunteers had cleared the backlog, there would be no ongoing work for them, often because staff were not prepared to relinquish the more interesting tasks. Sometimes, volunteers would turn up and find no one would give them any work at all, even though staff were rushed off their feet. This resulted in a downward spiral. Volunteer attendance became sporadic and staff complained about how unreliable volunteers were. Many volunteers left after only a few weeks, feeling annoyed at the cavalier way their contribution had been treated. Staff were fed up at having to re-start the process of bringing in new volunteers, getting to know them and explaining what had to be done. Over time staff made even less effort to induct new volunteers. 'Why bother?' they would say. 'They are only going to leave in a few weeks.'

Putting together a strategy for the overall volunteer programme might sound daunting but it doesn't need to be. It can begin by simply taking a look at the current involvement of volunteers. What works, and what is proving less successful? Where can you make improvements and how will you introduce the changes? Think about the future and ask yourself if there are any new areas where volunteers could be involved, or whether there are some existing areas where fewer volunteers are needed. Based on this work you can then set some objectives for yourself for the next year or two, and work out an action plan that breaks these objectives down into prioritised activities.

It is well worth taking time to build commitment to your plan from those within the organisation. By presenting your strategy to your manager, trustees and colleagues (including existing volunteers, if appropriate) you will have the opportunity to talk with them about the bigger picture. Getting their 'buy-in' for your plan is more likely to lead to their cooperation and support when it comes to implementing it.

The volunteer programme and your organisation

It is important to plan your volunteer programme in the context of the strategy for your organisation as a whole.

> Kathy, the volunteer coordinator of a children's voluntary organisation, heard in a staff meeting that the organisation had been awarded a grant to develop a project to support child carers. She was disappointed to hear about this project so late in the day as she thought volunteers could have made a significant contribution. It meant that she had missed the opportunity to include a budget for volunteers in the grant application, and there was therefore no money allocated to pay for the recruitment, training, supervision and expenses of new volunteers.

For an organisation to function effectively the different parts need to coordinate, complement and communicate with each other. Given that volunteers contribute to meeting your organisation's overall goals, your volunteer strategy won't be effective unless it is guided by the strategic plan for the whole organisation.

This requires the senior management team to inform the volunteer coordinator about their plans and to involve him or her in discussions about the ways in which volunteers can contribute to meeting the aims of the organisation. Equally, the volunteer coordinator needs to keep senior managers up to date about new plans and initiatives for making more effective use of volunteers. By including a plan for the volunteer programme in the organisation's overall strategy, volunteer involvement will always be part of your organisation's discussions about the future.

> When a leading campaigning organisation decided to restructure their staff teams, no thought was given to the implications for existing volunteers. Whole departments were broken up and formed into new units, and the job descriptions of many staff members were changed significantly. During the first week after restructuring, volunteers turned up for work and had no idea where to go. They didn't know whether to stay with the staff members they had worked with before, or go to the new department that most closely resembled their previous one. Some of the departments' functions had changed so radically it was hard to tell who did what any more, and the staff were too preoccupied trying to understand their new roles to think about the volunteers. The message this sent to the current volunteers was that they weren't needed, and many of them left – even though there was plenty of work for them.

Why do some organisations fail to integrate a plan for the volunteer programme into their overall strategic thinking? One reason is that those in charge view the work of volunteers as a 'nice' additional activity within the organisation, but not one that is crucial to its long-term success. A tell-tale sign of this attitude can be seen when the volunteer coordinator is not line managed by a director but by a supervisor lower down the hierarchy – in some cases in a role with no obvious link to voluntarism.

Volunteer coordinators have told us of their success at improving dialogue with their bosses on strategic issues by taking the following initiatives:

■ kicking off discussions about planning issues themselves and not waiting for their senior managers to do it;
■ preparing a strategic plan for their volunteer programme and asking the leaders to meet and discuss it;
■ requesting to be line managed in a more appropriate part of the organisation;
■ asking to be included in relevant teams that deal with planning issues;
■ publicising, in staff meetings, the annual report, newsletters, website, local press etc., the contribution that volunteers make to the organisation;
■ facilitating a discussion with managers on why the organisation involves volunteers, and how they contribute to achieving its aims.

Develop a policy on recruitment procedures

Agreeing a clear policy on volunteer involvement is another good way of engaging those at the top of your organisation in a discussion about the role of volunteers. There are, however, other significant benefits that arise from it.

A good policy will not only explain 'best practice' *guidelines* but will describe the *values* (or principles) that drive these procedures. It will help you to shape your approach to recruitment and, having gained the backing of your managers and trustees, you will know what you can realistically promise potential volunteers. Volunteers will certainly appreciate knowing that the same rules of the game apply to everyone.

A volunteer policy will cover not only your procedures relating to recruitment, although that is what we are focussing on here. It is likely that it will also cover selection procedures, support and supervision, equal opportunities, health and safety, insurance, discipline and grievance, confidentiality and so on. Whether all of these issues are covered in one almighty policy, or in a series of individual ones, is up to you. If you are interested in seeing some examples of volunteer policies, or would like some guidance on drawing up your own, contact the National Centre for Volunteering (see *Useful Addresses*).

The policy issues discussed below are particularly relevant to volunteer recruitment.

Why do you involve volunteers?

If you, and your colleagues, can't give a clear answer to this question, how can you be sure that your organisation believes in the value and benefits of working with volunteers? The answer here is not simply 'to save money'. While in many organisations volunteers are a financial necessity, their labour is not the only benefit they bring. The reasons that some organisations choose to involve volunteers can include:

- they are essential in building links with your service-users or supporters;
- they bring in fresh ideas and enthusiasm;
- they retain a neutrality between clients and staff;
- they complement the skills that staff possess;
- they have direct experience of the issues that your organisation seeks to address;
- they bring in new perspectives to the organisation's thinking;
- they help you build links with the local community;
- clients appreciate the support of a person who expects nothing in return.

Being clear about the 'added value' that volunteers bring to your organisation will help you and your colleagues to be enthusiastic about their involvement. But if you are apathetic about working with volunteers, how are you going to convince them to join you? If they mean nothing more to you than a means of balancing the budget they will quickly sense your lack of commitment to support them in their work.

Who can volunteer with you?

Some organisations have a policy of welcoming anybody who wants to volunteer with them and will, if no suitable roles are available, tailor one around the individual.

Most organisations, however, set certain limitations on who can volunteer. These most frequently relate to the skills, qualities and experience required to fulfil each volunteer role. In some cases there may be gender or age limitations for particular areas of work.

There may also be a number of general limitations applying to all volunteers. Examples that we've encountered include: members of the management committee cannot assume an additional volunteer role; a member of an employee's family cannot volunteer; no current or former clients can volunteer; and all volunteers have to fulfil certain health criteria. (Where these rules exist there is a good reason for them and they are not generic rules that any organisation should adopt as a matter of form.) Any such rules that exist in your organisation will obviously have an impact on how you go about recruiting volunteers.

We recommend that you don't set an upper age limit for volunteers, as it is discriminatory. A volunteer's ability to fulfil a role shouldn't be determined by their age but by whether they have the necessary skills, qualities or experience. However, you need to check whether your insurance company sets any age limitations on volunteers.

Legal restrictions on volunteering

There are fairly few legal restrictions these days on volunteering and the rules for benefit claimants and asylum seekers, in particular, have relaxed in recent times. You can find details of these – as well as guidelines on recruiting children and young people, those with criminal records, or people from outside the UK – in Appendix 1.

Equal opportunities

Equal opportunities (EO) involves addressing differences such as race, disability, gender, age, sexuality and so on, and taking steps to ensure that no volunteers are disadvantaged because of them. An equal opportunities policy fights discrimination, both direct (where individuals are treated differently under similar circumstances) and indirect (applying a rule which adversely affects volunteers from a particular group without good reason).

If you already have an EO policy for employees, then you could expand it to cover volunteers. In our experience many voluntary organisations still neglect to develop practical EO guidelines.

You can find a sample EO policy in Appendix 2. Once you have such a policy in place then you will need to consider its implications for the way you recruit volunteers. Do you use recruitment methods that exclude certain sectors of society? How can you direct your recruitment activity at groups who are under-represented in your organisation?

The recruitment process

This part of your policy should describe how you develop roles for volunteers, who is involved or consulted, and whether written role descriptions and person specifications are required. Is a risk assessment needed for each volunteering role, and if so how will the outcome of it affect your recruitment and selection procedures? Who is responsible for recruitment and who else is involved in the recruitment, selection and induction process? What are your response times for answering enquiries, getting back to people after interviews and so on?

Selection, induction and support of volunteers

While these areas are not the focus of this book, it's important to stress that not only will you want to include guidelines about them in your volunteer policy, but you will also need to ensure that the procedures are in place before you begin recruiting volunteers. There is little point in orchestrating a fabulous recruitment campaign if the follow-up is chaotic or ill thought out. You can read more about these issues in *Essential Volunteer Management* by Steve McCurley and Rick Lynch (see *Further Reading*).

Be clear about who you want to recruit

Buying a gift for someone whose tastes and interests you don't know is difficult. It's easy to come home either empty handed or with so many gifts that you can't choose between them. If you set out feeling unclear about who you want to recruit, you have as much chance of successfully finding volunteers as you have of getting that gift.

Devising roles for volunteers

The most important piece of planning you can do prior to recruitment is devising roles for volunteers. Not only do you need to be clear on what you want volunteers to do in each role, but you also have to think through the particular skills and qualities needed to do that work.

Clarity about each volunteer role – and the kind of people required to fill them – will help you determine how to set about finding your volunteers. The way you recruit a volunteer to design a website will be very different from finding someone suitable to befriend a family in need.

Clearly defined roles are helpful for volunteers too. They want to know beforehand what they are getting involved in, and what is going to be expected of them. A written role description will reassure them that you are well organised and that you are not going to waste their time. And by clearly stating in a person specification the kind of people you are looking for, prospective volunteers can more easily decide whether or not to apply.

By giving a written role description to each volunteer you will prevent misunderstandings about the nature of the voluntary work. While you may have made it clear in your recruitment campaign that you are looking for, say, mentors or fundraisers, people will have very different ideas about what these roles involve – not least because they differ from organisation to organisation. The distinction between the work that volunteers and employees do will also become more apparent, and this can be an important step in building the trust of staff who work alongside volunteers.

The process of writing down each volunteer role can be very useful in assessing the risks attached to people volunteering. Whether these are risks to which volunteers are exposed in the course of their work, or risks that they themselves might present to the organisation, staff, clients (or each other), you cannot undertake an effective risk assessment process without well-written role descriptions. It is only when you have thought through in detail the actions that a volunteer is likely to take in the course of their work that you can pinpoint the areas of risk.

Why 'role' descriptions?

As you've probably realised, role descriptions for volunteers are cousins of the job descriptions given to employees (although not usually written in the same style). For a while the term 'job description' was used with volunteers as well, but has recently fallen out of favour. It blurs the line between staff and volunteers, which can be confusing and, in a very small number of cases, legally problematic. Organisations have therefore sought an alternative term and 'role description' is one of the most commonly used. However, you can call it what you like – volunteer specification, task description, volunteer briefing, role definition or whatever. We've yet to find a term we really like, but what you call it is much less important than how you use it to help you plan and communicate your needs. For ease of writing, where we use the term 'role description', we assume it also includes a person specification.

Some people have concerns about giving volunteers defined roles on paper. They worry that volunteering could become too formal, too inflexible, and that people might be scared off. These concerns are not unrealistic, but they are not an effective argument against having role descriptions. Rather, they relate to issues on how they are used – whether the language is unfriendly or dogmatic, or whether or not the organisation is prepared to adapt and change a person's role over time. These are easily overcome.

In fact the biggest drawback in using role descriptions is the amount of time it takes to produce them. This is especially true if you have volunteers working in a wide range of roles, or if you create new roles around individual volunteer's skills. The key question, however, is whether you can afford *not* to write role descriptions. The benefits far outweigh the drawbacks – the time it takes to write them is less than that taken up with solving the problems caused by their absence. Role descriptions are, by far, the single biggest building block you can use to create thorough planning.

There are occasionally some volunteer tasks that don't merit a full role description. Where volunteers help with a one-off simple task – such as a sponsored walk – a full role description would be overkill. However you will still need to think about how you pass on instructions and guidelines to such volunteers.

How to write effective role descriptions

It is useful to have a template for writing role descriptions. Define what you feel is the minimum you expect for each role and consider what could be added once volunteers become more experienced. Keep it as brief as possible, as few people want to absorb more than one side of A4.

The outline below provides a template you can use and adapt to create your own volunteer role descriptions.

Role description template
Role title:
Purpose of role: *(why is role important?)*
Brief description of main tasks and activities:
Skills, experiences and qualities required: *(this is the person specification)*
Time commitment:
Support offered: *(such as expenses, training, support sessions etc.)*
Other commitments: *(e.g. any requirement to attend induction, training, support sessions, meetings etc.)*

You may meet some resistance in introducing role descriptions from volunteers who have been involved with your organisation for some time. Understanding why they oppose this change is important. They can easily feel unappreciated for the work they have already been doing – the role description may be perceived to imply criticism of them. They might also be concerned that the work will change and they won't be able (or willing) to adapt.

Take time to explain why there is a need to write role descriptions. It helps to give external reasons, such as insurance company requirements, health and safety laws (duty of care), or to give prospective volunteers further information about the role before joining. You can also describe how writing a role description helps you to plan recruitment and reduce levels of turnover.

Designing roles that motivate volunteers

Research shows that those organisations offering a variety of roles are amongst the most successful in engaging volunteers. A choice of roles also encourages people to stay longer. If you currently offer only a limited choice of work to volunteers, you might consider the following approaches to designing new roles.

Begin by getting a group of staff and/or volunteers together to list ideas for additional tasks that volunteers could do or new services they could provide. You could also survey your clients, members or supporters and ask them what their most important needs are.

A particularly useful exercise is to meet individually with staff and encourage them to identify areas of work where they feel under pressure or would find it helpful to have some assistance. Below is an exercise you can use to encourage staff to think about new ways they could work with volunteers.

Process to help identify new volunteer roles

1   Keep a log of all the tasks you undertake in a full week
2   Mark each task in one of the following ways:
    *** You could easily delegate this to a volunteer(s)
    ** You could do this together with a volunteer(s)
    * You don't want to (or it would be inappropriate) to delegate this to volunteers.
    Feel free to leave unmarked any that you can't decide about for the time being – but try and return to them soon
3   Finally, think about those tasks and activities that you would like done, but have neither the time nor resources for. Which of these could volunteers do?

Adapted from *Building Staff/Volunteer Relations*, by Ivan H. Scheier, Energize, Inc. 1993

Using the newly identified tasks that arise from these exercises you can shape new role descriptions for volunteers – or adapt existing ones to make them more varied and interesting.

Can you create any 'virtual' voluntary roles? Work that volunteers can do at home on their own computer is becoming more popular. These kinds of roles are attractive to volunteers because they can be easily fitted around other commitments. As well as obvious roles, such as website design and maintenance, volunteers are now providing services such as mentoring or counselling by e-mail.

Setting recruitment goals

What would you do if you had more free time? Many of us have activities or projects in the back of our minds that we'd like to get around to one day. It might be anything from decorating a room to learning the tango (go on, you know you want to really), reading a novel you bought ages ago, or simply catching up with an old friend. Somehow or other, though, we never do many of the things we dream about. Other commitments always seem to get in the way.

When it comes to managing volunteers it is equally easy for other responsibilities to squeeze recruitment off your agenda. No matter how much you want to get a recruitment drive up and running, getting around to doing it can be hard.

Setting goals is a proven and key way to help you move from daydreams to action. A well-written goal will give your recruitment a sense of urgency, and help to focus your mind and actions on getting the job done. And by building a timescale into your goal, you will give yourself a deadline to aim for.

With clearly defined goals in place, it is easier to work out the steps you need to take to recruit your volunteers. You'll also find you can communicate your plans to your colleagues much more clearly, which is particularly helpful if you rely on their commitment and support.

Goals are only effective if you keep them in front of you and review them regularly. Simply writing them, only to stuff them in the back of the filing cabinet, will mean you don't get the benefit of them. Review them on a weekly basis, otherwise you will quickly find that other pressures push them off your 'to-do' list.

Producing a well-formed recruitment goal

Implementing a recruitment plan involves beginning with the end in mind. To succeed in getting the volunteers you want, you will need to know exactly what you're aiming for. By writing down a goal you will create a springboard for your planning. Answering the following questions will help you to produce a goal that is well formed, specific and clearly defined:

1   **What do you want to achieve by recruiting volunteers?**
    As a first step, simply write down whatever comes into your mind in answer to this question.
2   **What, specifically, do you want to achieve?**
    Review your answer to question 1, but this time be more precise. In which parts of the organisation do you want volunteers? Who will they work with? What will they do, what are their responsibilities? What skills, experience and

qualities will they have? How many do you need? When do you want them by? It is crucial to formulate your goals in a positive way – you won't be motivated by a goal that is negatively expressed, such as 'We don't want volunteers who only stay for a few weeks'. While it can be useful to think about what you *don't* want, you should translate it into positive terms. So, 'We don't want volunteers who only stay for a few weeks' would become 'We will recruit volunteers who can commit for a year'.

3   Is your recruitment goal realistic?

Do you have the resources and time to achieve your goal? Do you have sufficient authority and control within the organisation to make it happen? Can you initiate it and carry it through? What do you need to help you achieve your goal? If you identify anything that will present an obstacle to achieving your goal you will either need to work out a way of removing it or else adjust your goal accordingly. Taking time at this stage to anticipate potential problems will boost your chances of achieving your goal and will remove frustration at a later date.

Anatomy of a recruitment goal

Here's an example of a well-formed recruitment goal, with some comments on the way it has been constructed:

We will recruit[1], by the end of April[2], twelve volunteers[3] with listening skills[4] who, between them[5] will provide forty hours[6] of staffing per week on our telephone helpline[7].

[1]The goal is expressed in positive terms

[2]A deadline is included to encourage timetabling the different stages of the recruitment plan

[3]Specific and quantifiable

[4]Adds detail about the kind of people being recruited. However, there is still flexibility about how these people are found – do they already have listening skills when they are recruited or will the organisation train them? Or a bit of both? These are questions that the plan can provide answers to

[5]More flexibility is built into the plan here. Not all volunteers need necessarily contribute the same amount of time each week, so long as between them they provide forty hours

[6]Another measurable aspect of the goal, this time in relation to the contribution the new volunteers will make to the organisation

[7]The goal describes specifically what the volunteers will do. Anybody reading this goal can quickly understand what the recruitment plan is setting out to do and the impact it will have on the organisation

4   **Does the goal fit in with your organisation?**
     This final stage of the goal setting process invites you to step back and see your goal in the context of the wider organisation. Does it fit in with your other plans for the volunteer programme? Does it avoid contradicting any other goals or values held by the wider organisation? What will happen when you achieve your goal – will you, or the organisation, lose anything by achieving it? Take time to check whether your goal is in harmony with the rest of your organisation's activities. If you don't, a problem is certain to present itself to you at a later stage – probably once you have already expended time and energy on working towards your goal.

Once you have your recruitment goals in place you are ready to begin work on deciding which recruitment methods you will choose to achieve them. Read on!

RECRUITING THE SKILLS YOU NEED

Recently, on television, one of our ubiquitous celebrity chefs accompanied a North Sea fishing crew on an overnight voyage to catch shrimp. It was dark by the time the boat reached its destination to lower its nets, and the sun had already risen when the crew hauled in their catch. Impressively, the nets were crammed with nothing but glistening pink shrimp. How do they do this? Why aren't the nets filled with a motley collection of fish, lobsters, squid, seaweed and bits of old oil rigs?

Fishing crews can't afford to take pot luck. They have to maximise their catch and get back to the fish market promptly, so they can't spend time sifting through a miscellaneous collection of sea life to identify what they want to keep and then throw back the rest. Years of fishing tradition and skill mean that trawler crews are able to set sail knowing exactly what they want to catch, where to find it, and when is the best time to haul it in.

So pull on your wellies and sou'westers and join us for 'The deep-sea fishers' guide to recruiting volunteers'.

Who do you want to catch?

If you have included a detailed person specification in the volunteer role description, you will already have a clearer idea of the kind of person you are looking for and the skills they need to possess.

Failure to define exactly the kind of person wanted will present a major hurdle for any volunteer recruiter. Some recruiters choose to avoid being too specific. They say, 'How can we be choosy when we are asking people to give their time and effort for nothing?' Or, 'It would be really good to have a volunteer who can do such and such but we'll never find anybody with that skill'. Or even, 'If they are so well skilled they are not going to want to help us for free'. It's as if these recruiters have told themselves that they are never going to find who they want and, even before they start recruiting, have already settled for 'making do' with whoever they can find. Their reluctance to be focussed virtually guarantees their failure to find the right people.

We'll spare you the sermon on positive thinking but take it from us, the only way you are going to catch shrimp is if you set out looking for shrimp. Otherwise you will be left trawling around half-heartedly in the nearest rock pool wondering how you can make use of a small crab and a couple of whelks.

The criteria in your person specification, however, may be quite detailed. If you have thought about the skills, experience, availability and personal attributes necessary for someone to do your voluntary work, your shopping list of requirements may well be too long for you realistically to find people who meet all of your criteria in one leap. Some prioritisation will be necessary, and you can sort your criteria under three headings:

- With which criteria will I start my search?
- Which criteria can potential volunteers assess themselves against?
- Which criteria can I leave until the selection stage?

With which criteria will I start my search?

Usually it will be easier and more effective to start your recruitment drive by focussing on one particular requirement. When your volunteers need to have a key skill, then this will normally be where your search begins and all your other criteria can be sorted under the remaining two headings. If you are looking for people who can garden, decorate, keep accounts, coach a sport, programme a computer, offer counselling and such like, then put this skill under your first heading.

If it is not a skill as such that you are looking for then you might identify which of your criteria is the most unusual or rare. For example, when Arthritis Care were recruiting volunteers to undertake advisory work, it was essential that they had experience of living with arthritis. This is not exactly a skill but is such a particular and unique factor in the person specification that it provides an excellent starting point for the recruitment campaign.

If you find that none of your recruitment criteria are particularly special or unique, nor relate to a key skill, you could review them to see if any could be made more specific. Alternatively, if you are seeking volunteers with particular qualities or attributes rather than skills or experience, the strategy discussed in this chapter may not be the most appropriate for you – Chapter 3 outlines another approach to recruitment that you may find more helpful.

Which criteria can potential volunteers assess themselves against?

The criteria that you put under your second heading are those factors that potential recruits can themselves use to determine their own suitability for volunteering. Having successfully got your recruitment message to people with the necessary skill, you leave them to opt out if they don't match your other requirements.

Availability is a good example of one such criterion – people can judge for themselves whether they have the time it takes to commit to your organisation. There is nothing especially unique about being available for, say, four hours a week, so you wouldn't seek people principally on the grounds of their free time when you have other criteria that are less easily met. But if you begin your recruitment drive by first finding people with the right skills you can then let them work out if they have the time. Other criteria you could list under this heading include the volunteer's motivation, their experience of the issues or needs that your organisation addresses, ability to travel, having their own car and so on.

We're not suggesting that the factors you put under this heading are less important than those under other headings, but that for the purposes of your recruitment strategy, it is more effective to leave these to the 'prospect' to decide. However, do keep these secondary criteria in mind when considering how you target people. You might, for example, want to avoid targeting full-time office workers if you need help during the day. Although they may have the necessary skills, they are obviously not available when you need them, and so there is no sense in your strategy targeting this group.

Which criteria can I leave until selection stage?

The criteria that you put under this third heading are those factors that are best left until the selection stage. These are the parts of the person specification that it would be extremely hard to assess people's suitability for at an earlier stage, but which are nonetheless important for the voluntary work. Often these will be personal qualities and attributes (such as being open-minded, non-judgemental, honest, caring or friendly) which you can assess at an interview or during induction training, or they may be checks for convictions, health and such like.

By prioritising your specification in this way, you are beginning to use your criteria strategically, and it will give your recruitment activity a focus rather than relying on taking a shot in the dark. Instead of trying to find people who meet all your criteria in one go, you are narrowing down the recruitment process in steps. With each step you move closer to your target. Or as our fishing crew might put it: you go to where the shrimp are and catch them, but you still throw back the ones that are too small.

Where to catch the volunteers you need

Pick up any book on starting a business and they invariably tell you that the three most important things to think about are location, location and location. This may be a cliché, but is no less true because of it. Although you are not starting a business you *are* looking for 'customers', which is why location is so important. Instead of marketing a product you are selling a volunteering opportunity – an idea we'll explore further in Chapter 4 – and to attract the right customers your recruitment message will need to be seen in all the right places.

Our friends on the high seas start fishing around in the places where they know that shrimps like to hang out. Volunteer recruiters who do little more than drop their nets in the nearest puddle are in for a long wait.

There are certain stereotyped methods of recruiting volunteers that have become strong cultural traditions in the voluntary sector. Classic examples include putting up a poster in the library, leaflets in the local GP's waiting room or an advert in the local paper. We've noticed how hard people find it to let go of these habits. But are these recruiters finding enough of the right volunteers? In the same way that a broken clock tells the right time twice a day, an advert in the local paper will always prompt the odd application or two. Yet if you are seeking people with particular skills, why direct your message at an audience where the majority doesn't meet your criteria? It is not a strategy that makes best use of your limited time and resources, and just because you were lucky with it once doesn't mean you will be again.

There are other ways to target more effectively people with the skills you are looking for. Try pulling together a few of your more imaginative colleagues and volunteers (they're the ones who recount the most outrageous exploits to you on a Monday morning, yet mysteriously look fresh as a daisy) for a brainstorming session (see Chapter 8, page 75) to come up with some ideas.

Collect suggestions of occupations or businesses in which people have the skills you need. Weed out those places where only a few of the employees have 'your' skill in favour of those where most of them do. For example, to find someone with computer skills you could target just about any business – after all most places now have at least one person on the staff who knows their ASCII from their elbow. But it would be more by chance than strategy that you'd successfully hook that one skilled person out of a pond of others. Instead, you can prioritise those occupations and businesses where most of the staff are computer literate: internet cafés, web design firms, computer sales centres, programmers, service and repair firms, IT consultants and such like. Your recruitment message will then reach a much higher proportion of people with the right skills.

Recruiting skilled people at their place of work is one way of reaching them, but you can also consider other points of contact they have – professional institutes, trade guilds, conferences, journals or trade magazines.

Targeting people on the basis of their occupation doesn't only mean reaching out to those who are currently employed in that field. Where are people being trained in the skills that you seek? Check out your local colleges and learning centres. You might also look for people who have retired from your target occupation. Admittedly, it is harder to find places where retired people, all with the skills you are looking for, congregate. However some employers have social clubs or leisure facilities which their retired staff continue to make use of, while others run pre-retirement courses for those who are about to give up work.

Elizabeth wanted to recruit two or three volunteers to help her produce regular newsletters and publicity materials for her organisation. The principal skill required was desktop publishing, and so she telephoned her local college and spoke to the administrator of the graphic design department. As a result Elizabeth was able to put a poster on the department's notice board, which yielded nearly a dozen replies. She now has three DTP volunteers who work with commitment and enthusiasm because of the freedom they have to utilise their skills and creativity, while at the same time building up a portfolio of work.

Recruiting people on the basis of occupation is a good starting place but it is not your only option. Identify locations where you will find a high concentration of the right people. Consider hobbies and leisure activities. Find gardeners in garden centres, football coaches at the sports centre, drivers at the car park, decorators at the DIY shop or arts and crafts people at local classes and workshops. Many enthusiasts now take part in internet user groups and discussion forums devoted to their interest, so why not log on and talk to them?

As well as finding people who already have the skills you need, also think about those who might like to acquire them. Do you have the capacity to train new volunteers in the necessary skill? In some cases it will obviously be impractical to consider this (e.g. driving) whereas with others – listening skills, counselling, conservation – the training you offer may be a big inducement for people. In this case, some of the criteria in your person specification will need to relate to the applicant's capacity and motivation to learn.

If you're feeling really creative, another approach is to think about transferable skills. What skills from a different setting could be transferred to yours? If you want public speakers, can you think of anyone who addresses people as part of their job or as a pastime – teachers, clergy, toastmasters? If you need volunteers to organise fundraising teams or events, who has good organisational skills?

When is a good time to catch people?

It is perhaps easier to think about this question in reverse – when are there bad times to recruit volunteers that you can avoid?

Don't ask people to volunteer when their mind is on something else. People are often preoccupied in the weeks running up to their summer holiday or in the run-up to Christmas. Many volunteer recruiters we have met tell us they avoid these times of year because they don't get such a good response. On the other hand, both September and January are times of the year when many people have a 'new start' or 'new term' frame of mind and may be thinking through some bigger questions about how they organise their lives. Maybe that is a better time to approach them. (Although some volunteer recruiters have told us that they have recruited very successfully over Christmas and summer, this seems to be the exception rather than the rule).

There are other occasions when people may be preoccupied. If you are contacting people at work, try and catch them at a time when they are not as busy or their mind isn't full of the day's tasks. Maybe lunchtime would be good? If you are stalking our green-fingered friends at the garden centre, catch them while they are browsing rather than at the checkout (where they are nervously wondering if the cashier will accept their credit card).

Whoever you decide to target with your recruitment message, give some thought as to when might be a bad time to approach them and work around it.

Where do you start?

The more ideas you generate about where to find people with the desired skills the more successful you are going to be. If you've been very imaginative, and come up with lots of possibilities, you will be faced with a decision about where to start. You probably won't have the time or resources to use all of your ideas, and even if you did, you might find more people volunteering than you can manage. (It happens!)

Deciding which of your ideas to use first calls for some careful judgement and you will have to accept that there may be some trial and error involved. Don't rule out your gut instinct. Which of your ideas excite you? Which suggestions surprised you with their simplicity or originality? Which feel daring and adventurous? If it feels like a good idea, give it a go.

You might also take time to reflect on your organisation's previous experience of recruiting volunteers. What strategies worked well in the past but are no longer successful? Why did they stop being effective and could they be adapted or varied to make them relevant again? What approaches to recruitment have always been disappointing? As you sort through your new ideas, build on the lessons your organisation has learned in the past and let go of those habits that no longer get results.

One final factor to think about when assessing your recruitment ideas is the motivation of those you want to recruit. Why would somebody in a particular occupation want to volunteer with you? In what way would it be rewarding or satisfying for them? Choose those recruitment ideas in which you can clearly see the benefits to the volunteer of getting involved – not only will they be more likely to sign up, but it will be easier for you to find ways of selling your volunteering opportunity to them.

RECRUITING THROUGH YOUR NETWORK

It is easy to assume that, to recruit enough volunteers, all you need do is spend enough on publicity. After all, if you could increase and improve your advertising and promotional materials, just think how many potential volunteers you could reach – if only you had the money.

The reality is that many voluntary organisations have very tight budgets for volunteer recruitment – if indeed they have a budget at all. Look at it this way: at least you have a good excuse for failing to find enough volunteers – it's not your fault, if only the trustees would allocate more money to the volunteer programme...

There is no doubt that advertising and publicity can be very effective in targeting appropriate people to volunteer. But according to the 1997 National Survey of Volunteering, published by the Institute for Volunteering Research, just under half of all volunteers are recruited because someone *personally* asked them to help. That is to say, a significant number of people are recruited through knowing someone in the organisation.

Who is in your network?

Here's an exercise you can try to test out the extent of your own network. Take a sheet of paper and write down all the numbers from one to a hundred. Next to each number write the name of somebody you know – friends, relations, neighbours, colleagues (current and former), club members, and so on. Think of absolutely everybody you are on speaking terms with. Can you fill the sheet? When you've finished, take a minute to consider whether any of these people might make a good volunteer. Have you ever asked them?

Recruitment by word of mouth

Experienced volunteer recruiters will not be surprised at the importance of personal contacts. Consider your own volunteer programme: how many volunteers got involved because they already had some contact with your organisation? The chances are that you probably have a fair few friends, spouses, relatives, neighbours and colleagues working together in your project. What they have in common is that they were part of your organisation's network, and along the way somebody roped them in.

A personal approach to recruitment is very powerful. It is the only recruitment strategy that confronts individuals with your need for help *and* demands a reply. Publicity only informs your audience that you need volunteers – it requires them to take the initiative to contact you. A personal request, on the other hand, reaches out directly and individually to the people you want. Publicity is passive; personal contact is active. It is impossible to ignore.

The power of the personal approach

Commercial organisations have long realised the value of word-of-mouth endorsements over other forms of advertising – more so as consumers become increasingly sophisticated. Nowadays, we take advertisers' claims about their products with a pinch of salt. But we will trust the opinions of our friends. Perhaps you can recall a time when you discovered a new shop, product or business that excited you and discussed it with your family or acquaintances. Or maybe you've been looking for a good plumber, mechanic or dentist and have asked around for a recommendation. Increasingly, marketing departments are trying to encourage us to 'talk up' their business to people we know. And when was the last time a sample of shampoo or cleaning product dropped through your letterbox? You try it, you like it, you talk about it. Of course, we'll only talk positively about those products and services that excite us. We will also talk to friends about bad experiences we've had and warn them about companies whose service disappointed, frustrated or angered us.

What kind of experience are you giving to your volunteers? Are they enthusiastic about your organisation? Will they talk with excitement about how satisfying it is to work with you?

Directly appealing to somebody for their help works because it surmounts some of the common barriers that discourage people from volunteering with you.

People like to be asked

Some folk would feel they were being 'pushy' if they nominated themselves as a volunteer. They would consider it an honour to be asked, but wouldn't dream of suggesting themselves. They think it would be impolite. This doesn't mean they aren't keen to help or lack the skills you're looking for. But when you tell a person you need them, it is more affirming and leaves them feeling that they are doing you a favour – not the other way around.

> When a local parish church was organising its spring fair, announcements by the vicar asking for helpers failed to recruit enough volunteers. Instead, the organiser approached particular people and asked them if they would do a specific job. She approached individuals on the basis of their interests and skills. A couple of people who enjoyed listening to music were asked to run the CD stall; an author and a keen reader organised the bookstall; and parents were approached to staff the toy stall. People were more than willing to help and were pleased to have been asked personally. All the jobs were covered and over £1000 was raised for church funds.

Not everyone feels confident to volunteer for you

To volunteer for a role in your organisation people need to have self-confidence. They have to believe they have the skills and abilities you're looking for. It will depend on the nature of the work just how much confidence is needed, but some people will tell themselves that they can't possibly do your job – even when it would be relatively easy for them. If you explain in person that you not only want them, but feel sure they would do a great job, then you invest them with the confidence they need. They don't have to generate it themselves.

Will new volunteers feel welcome?

Some volunteers are shy of going into situations where they don't know anybody. Will they be welcomed or made to feel an outsider? Will people be supportive and encouraging, or demanding and thoughtless? Others may have had bad experiences of volunteering, where they were made to feel second class. Your voluntary work may sound worthwhile and interesting but some people won't want to take the risk. When a friend is already involved in your organisation, however, and asks them to help out, they can be sure of at least one friendly face. And maybe their friend will convince them that the rest of you aren't too bad either.

Are you a credible organisation?

If you are recruiting for Oxfam, the Red Cross or the RSPCA then there is a good chance that prospective volunteers will already have heard of you, know something of your work and have formed a view about whether they like you or not. But what if you are recruiting for the Auchtermuchty Donkey Sanctuary, or the Grimsby Environmental Trust? If I've never heard of you how do I know if you are a credible, well-organised and professional organisation or a bunch of well-intentioned but shambolic do-gooders? If you are relatively unknown, recruiting through your network of contacts can reassure people that you are a worthwhile organisation to be involved with (unless you actually *are* a bunch of shambolic eccentrics, in which case you're going to need more than this book to help you...)

Finding the personalities you're looking for

For some voluntary roles (such as befrienders, buddies or mentors) the key attributes people need often centre less on skills and more on personality. It is very difficult to target a recruitment campaign at people who are patient, caring, warm or friendly in the way that you might look for people with, say, book-keeping experience or gardening skills. Recruiting through word of mouth can mobilise your network to identify prospective volunteers with the qualities and people skills you're looking for.

Mobilising your staff, volunteers, trustees and members

An additional benefit of getting others to find volunteers for you is that recruitment becomes a shared responsibility. Instead of it simply being down to the volunteer coordinator, everyone can get involved. For this to work you will need to support and encourage your existing network of staff, volunteers, trustees, members, supporters – and possibly even service-users – to recruit others. Here are some ways to do this.

Share the responsibility with volunteers

Involve existing volunteers in developing your recruitment strategy. Ask for their ideas and input when developing roles and considering methods of finding new volunteers. Aim to give your current volunteers a sense of ownership for the volunteer programme. Include responsibility for recruitment in their own role descriptions, and emphasise during their induction how vital their help can be in keeping the volunteer programme well staffed.

Give volunteer recruitment a high profile

Give regular feedback to your volunteers, staff and other members about your recruitment needs and share your successes with them. Use team meetings and newsletters to maintain a high awareness about recruitment. Publish your targets and deadlines to remind people continually that they can help by thinking of people who might volunteer. Put up posters and notices in places where your colleagues loiter (photocopier, kettle, toilets!) to remind them to recruit for you. Change your notices regularly to keep the message fresh and be creative, imaginative and fun in the way you put it across.

Offer resources and opportunities to support recruitment

Produce leaflets or information packs that people can pass on to their contacts. Hold open days where members can bring friends along to find out more about your organisation's work. Offer one-off activities, such as a sponsored walk, that your people can ask their friends to help with, and then follow up these new contacts to ask if they would like to volunteer more regularly. Encourage work shadowing so that potential volunteers can come along and observe their friend volunteering. Run a thank-you party for your volunteers during Volunteers' Week and encourage them to bring someone along to see how enjoyable it is to be part of your organisation. Consider what rewards or incentives you could give to people who successfully introduce a new volunteer to the organisation. Work out the financial value of a volunteer's work (hourly rate for an employee in that role multiplied by number of hours worked per year) to remind people how much they are giving to the organisation when they find a new volunteer for you.

Present your request positively

The way in which people are asked to volunteer can make quite a difference to their response, so consider giving guidance to people on how to present their request. Encourage your recruiters to be upbeat and positive about your organisation. Present volunteering as an opportunity to make a real difference to the work you do. Don't say that you are desperate for help – it is hardly a compliment to the person being asked. You want them to feel that it is an honour to have been invited to volunteer! Succinctly, introduce your organisation's purpose, the difference that your existence makes and the impact of your volunteers' contribution. Be knowledgeable about the role (or the choice of roles) for which you are inviting prospective volunteers to apply. Make it clear to them why you think they would be useful and what they might get out of volunteering for you. Be direct, honest and positive when making your request but avoid 'overselling' the voluntary work. Don't be pushy, and be gracious if the person declines your invitation. Even if they say 'no' you will still have one extra person who knows more about your organisation than before.

Who are your 'broadcasters'?

Identify people in your organisation's network who are in a good position to broadcast your need for volunteers. If one of your trustees is married to a lecturer at a local college, ask them to promote your need for volunteers among suitable students. If one of your volunteers also works for a big employer, involve them in setting up an employer-supported volunteering scheme. Who in your organisation belongs to a club, society or place of worship that could encourage their membership to volunteer with you? Learn as much as you can about your organisation's network of contacts and make the most of every opportunity to recruit through it.

Checklist for recruiting through your network

1   Think of the different groups that make up the network of people involved in your organisation. For example, trustees, staff, volunteers, service-users, members, supporters, funders, agencies – who else can you think of?
2   How can you involve each of these groups in recruiting volunteers?
3   What type of support and materials do these different groups need to encourage them to recruit for you?
4   Who can help you in supporting the different groups to recruit volunteers?

Common pitfalls in word-of-mouth recruitment

As we've seen, recruiting by word of mouth is cheaper, less time consuming and more effective than publicity. To make it work will require a good deal of thought and dedication. However, there are also some drawbacks to this type of recruitment which your strategy should take account of.

Like attracts like

If you want to improve the diversity of volunteers in your programme – to gain a wider spread of ages, gender, ethnic background and so on – then recruiting solely through your organisation's personal contacts may not help you to achieve it. On the whole, an organisation that consists largely of, say, older women will tend to attract more of the same if they are reaching out to their friends to find new volunteers. When people invite their contacts to volunteer they are already engaging in a form of selection. Not only are they likely to consider those people they know are capable of doing the job, but also those with whom they feel comfortable or get on easily. In many cases these will be people like themselves. To increase diversity, use other forms of recruitment to target those sectors of society that are under-represented in your organisation. Once you are happy with the mix, then word-of-mouth recruitment should help you to maintain it.

Betty, a retired schoolteacher, saw an advert appealing for volunteers to help a talking newspaper scheme. She had the time to spare and she was confident she also had the necessary skills. As well as having to speak clearly in the classroom, Betty had studied elocution and knew she would be able to articulate clearly enough to record articles from the local newspaper onto cassette for visually impaired listeners. She applied as a volunteer and was accepted. The project's recruitment advert failed to find enough other volunteers so Betty set about asking people she knew to help out. She only considered asking those people whom she knew had time to spare and had a good speaking voice. As a result Betty recruited another four volunteers – all of whom were retired colleagues from her teaching days. Her experience demonstrated the effectiveness of using personal contacts to recruit volunteers over advertising. It also followed the convention that like attracts like.

Bust those cliques

Another danger of recruiting through your network, particularly if your organisation is quite small, is that the volunteer programme can become 'clubby' if too many people are drawn from the same circle of friends. Once cliques get a foothold in your volunteer programme, it becomes much harder for those outside of it to break in and feel welcome. If you see this beginning to happen, ensure you use a variety of recruitment methods to help you draw from a wider range of people.

Maintain your selection procedures

When encouraging members of your organisation to seek new volunteers, make sure they are clear that they are inviting their contacts to *apply* to become a volunteer. Avoid misunderstandings where potential volunteers assume that, because a friend is already involved, they will automatically be accepted. If you normally interview volunteers, take up references or have pre-appointment training, make it clear in advance that everyone has to go through these procedures. Ill feeling can arise, both on the part of the applicant and the person who invited them along, if you turn down the new volunteer because they are unsuitable. Include a clear person specification in the volunteer's role description so applicants understand that you are looking for more than someone with a friend in your organisation.

Are your volunteers enjoying themselves?

Your volunteers will talk with enthusiasm about your organisation to their friends and family provided they are having a good time. Is volunteering well organised, satisfying and rewarding? Or is there low morale and a high turnover of volunteers? If your existing volunteers are grumbling or unhappy, now may not be the best time to encourage them to recruit for you. Work at making volunteering with your organisation a positive experience, and word-of-mouth recruitment will flow much more easily.

Jagdish was employed as a fundraising coordinator for an aid agency that supported projects in developing countries. Through his work with the charity, his family got to hear about the difference the agency was making to the lives of some of the world's poorest people. Jagdish's mother, sister and mother-in-law all volunteered to organise fundraising in the towns where they lived. Jagdish worked with the agency for six years before moving on to a new role in another charity, but his family continued to do their voluntary work. Ten years later, they are still at it and have raised tens of thousands of pounds for projects overseas. Without Jagdish realising it, his enthusiasm for the organisation that employed him turned him into an effective ambassador for their cause, and in the process led to the recruitment of volunteers who have, between them, contributed over 45 years of service.

Don't blame the trustees!

Before committing your time and effort to expensive publicity, take time to consider whether you have fully utilised your organisation's existing network of contacts to recruit new volunteers. And if your trustees won't cough up the cash for that glitzy multi-media recruitment campaign you've been dreaming about, don't forget that you have a cheaper option to pursue, which may well be more successful.

chapter 4

RECRUITMENT MESSAGES THAT GET RESULTS

Advertising has become a very sophisticated process. These days the link between product and message isn't as clear as it once was. On television, a woman taming some wolves promotes a famous French perfume. A surreal sequence involving a man clambering over a mob to look through a peephole at squirrels is about beer – obviously! And a tank of swimming goldfish has something to do with financial services. We *think*.

These type of ads don't aim to tell us much about the product itself. Instead, they are attempting to build 'brand consciousness'. They want to remind us that the product exists and aim to build positive associations with it in our minds.

Many other adverts do still speak directly to us about the product and try to persuade us of the benefits of buying it. Advertisers have been using the same formula to construct these messages since the end of the nineteenth century. Although watching re-runs of old television adverts – with their outdated values and patronising voiceovers in clipped accents – is the cause of much amusement these days, they are not so far removed in design from many of today's commercials. Soap powder ads have most obviously kept to this formula.

> 'Can't get your whites really clean? New improved Splodge is our best ever powder. With its powerful additional stain-removing ingredient, new Splodge can get rid of even the toughest stains. Now you can get great results wash after wash. So next time you want your whites *really* white, use new improved Splodge.'

You've seen this ad in various forms hundreds of times, and it is most commonly still in use for shampoos, nappies, cosmetics, sanitary and cleaning products.

The advertising formula

The formula that is used to construct these commercials is known as AIDA, an acronym that stands for:

A = Awareness

I = Interest

D = Desire

A = Action

It is designed to provide a logical sequence of thinking that consumers are taken through, starting with getting their attention and ending with them rushing out to buy the product. You can see how the formula is used to break down the advert for our fictitious soap powder:

Awareness: 'Can't get your whites really clean? New improved Splodge is our best ever powder.'
(The advert presents a problem with which consumers can identify, and makes them aware that a new product is on the market which will solve this problem.)

Interest: 'With its powerful additional stain-removing ingredient, new Splodge can get rid of even the toughest stains.'
(Here's what's interesting about our new product – a new ingredient. Wow!)

Desire: 'Now you can get great results wash after wash.'
(This is the bit where the consumer is shown the results of using the new product, to motivate them to use it.)

Action: 'So next time you want your whites *really* white, use new improved Splodge.'
(The advertiser tells the consumer what they should do next. Buy some.)

When it comes to recruiting volunteers the same formula can be equally effective. Although you are not selling a product you are selling a volunteering opportunity, and you will need to try and engage your audience in much the same way.

Awareness

What does your audience need to know about your organisation before they will consider volunteering with you?

The answer is not 'We need volunteers'. This is the least interesting thing about you as far as the public is concerned. And yet we see scores of adverts that start with the words 'Volunteers needed'. This is an easy trap to fall into, but it fails to get into the mind of your audience because it talks to them only from your own perspective. Messages like these often follow the same pattern: 'We need volunteers; the kind of work we do is [blah blah]; the kind of people we need are [such and such]'.

There is nothing in this approach which tries to engage volunteers from their standpoint. Nan Hawthorne, Editor-in-Chief of *Volunteer Management Review* (an American e-Newsletter, see *Useful Addresses*) likens this to a restaurant putting a sign in its window saying 'Eat here – we need to sell some food'. As a hungry customer you are not interested in what the restaurant needs. You want to know if the food tastes good and if you can afford it. As Hawthorne points out, a restaurant using this approach would sound desperate – not unlike a recruitment ad headed 'Volunteers desperately needed'. People reading that, she says, 'are thinking "Why? What's wrong with what they want volunteers to do?"'

Creating awareness begins by telling your audience about your work. Particularly if they have never heard of you, they need to know about what you do and why you do it. In *Essential Volunteer Management* (see *Further Reading*) Steve McCurley and Rick Lynch suggest you start by describing the difference your organisation makes. 'Most recruiting messages seldom talk about why you want the person to do a particular job,' they write. 'They only talk about the activities the person will be performing. This leaves it up to the person being recruited to figure out what the need for those activities is.'

By starting with a 'statement of the need' as they describe it, you will cut right to the heart of why volunteering with you is important and create awareness of what your organisation's purpose truly is.

A good example of this appeared in a recent ad by Friends United Network. It began by saying 'Some children really need the undivided attention of an adult who cares'. In a sentence they convey that volunteering with them is important, not because their organisation needs you, but because their clients do.

Compare this to an advert currently being run by another organisation. '[We are] the UK's largest voluntary provider of breaks for carers and disabled people,' it begins. While this is an impressive claim, the reader is left to deduce why giving carers and disabled people a break is necessary. If you have no experience of being either a carer or disabled it may be hard to understand why this voluntary work is so important.

The difference between the first ad and the second is that the Friends United Network talk about their service-users – and therefore their purpose – while the other organisation tells you about itself. In fairness to the latter, so do many other voluntary organisations but it can create an unnecessary hurdle in the reader's understanding of your work.

Whether you are a charity, campaigning group or membership organisation, begin your recruitment message by telling the audience the difference you make to people's lives, your cause or to your members.

'As well as deepening their interest in the work, this type of approach also reassures prospective volunteers that the work they will do really does make an important difference to the life of your service-users or to the success of your campaign.'

Why 'Would you like to volunteer?' doesn't work

In our minds there is only one thing worse than beginning your recruitment message with 'Volunteers wanted,' and that is the plethora of messages currently in circulation that begin with the words 'Would you like to volunteer?' – or similar variations. There are three reasons for avoiding this approach:

1   Too many other organisations use it and your message won't stand out from theirs. We recently saw a volunteering noticeboard on which well over half of the posters were headed with this question, making it impossible for readers to identify quickly the organisation that might interest them. Why not try something original?

2   When we see the question 'Would you like to volunteer?' the first answer that usually comes to mind is 'No'. People are probably not thinking about volunteering when they see your message – they're deciding what to have for dinner or worrying about their leaky roof. An effective ad or poster doesn't assume that people are considering volunteering when they start reading it, but aims to make sure they are by the time they've finished

3   It is a volunteer recruiter's fantasy that great herds of the British public are milling about with time on their hands looking for things to do. In fact, people who are employed or in full-time study are statistically more likely to volunteer than retired or unemployed people. It is often the busy people who find a way of squeezing voluntary work into their lives. A good recruitment message will aim to persuade people that it is worthwhile taking on a volunteer role.

Interest

Having caught your audience's attention by telling them about the need your organisation addresses, continue to engage their interest by explaining *how* you meet that need. In particular, tell them about the work that your volunteers do and the impact it has on your clients or cause.

Consider the ways in which you can help potential volunteers understand the connection between the work you want them to do and the needs of your service-users or campaign.

The New Bridge is an organisation that recruits and trains volunteers to write to, visit and befriend prisoners. Their recruitment materials explain well the need that volunteers meet and the impact they have on their service-users:

'Many prisoners never receive letters or visits, yet everyone needs someone to be interested in them and with whom they can talk things over; someone they can trust and who is independent of the Prison Service.'

Quotes from prisoners, such as the one below, are used to describe the value of volunteers' work:

'My voluntary Associate has given me the courage to look forward to the future. His friendship and trust has helped me to see where I have gone wrong in the past. I shall never ever come back to prison again.'

The leaflet also reinforces the wider benefits of the work that The New Bridge's volunteers undertake: 'You may be taking the first step in preventing further crime and so lessening the number of future victims, for the majority of crime is committed by the same small percentage of people, many of whom may be sent to prison again and again.'

Christian Aid Week falls in the middle of May each year. The focus of the week is a fundraising initiative where volunteers distribute collection envelopes through their neighbours' letterboxes, and return to pick up the donations later in the week. In 2000, 300,000 volunteers raised £12 million for Christian Aid's work in some of the world's poorest countries.

Given the scale of this annual event, Christian Aid always needs to supplement their core of regular collectors. In recent years they have used an imaginative word-of-mouth recruitment strategy – they distribute a video to their network of supporters, volunteers and churches. The video uses footage of Christian Aid's work abroad to explain how the money is used and to show the difference that it makes to people's lives. It is an extremely effective way of creating interest in volunteering for the organisation by linking the voluntary work with those who benefit from it overseas. As well as helping to create interest among new volunteers, the video also helps to retain the interest and motivation of regular collectors.

Try and mention some of the specific tasks and activities that your volunteers do so that your audience can begin to build a picture of what volunteering with you is like. Rather than just talking about roles – befriender, fundraiser, trustee, shop worker, administrator – briefly describe what that work involves. Don't assume your audience will draw the right conclusions about what these terms mean.

It will also help if each recruitment message focuses on a particular role, rather than trying to explain the range of roles available in your organisation. This will give your message a clarity that potential volunteers will relate to more easily.

It is much easier to explain the link between the voluntary work and the needs of your clients, members or campaign if the work that your volunteers do is front line. People can immediately appreciate the importance of a volunteer who is offering telephone counselling to depressed and suicidal callers, or delivering meals on wheels to older people at home. In these cases, the work of the volunteers *is* the work of the organisation.

Many volunteers, however, work in support roles such as administration, fundraising, running shops, committee members and so on. Strictly speaking, the needs met by these volunteers are principally *internal* to the organisation and have a secondary impact on those who benefit from your work. But people won't be very interested to hear the work they do described merely as help to those who do the *really* important work! You still need to find a way of linking the work volunteers do in secondary roles to your front line work.

UNICEF (United Nations Children's Fund) illustrates the point well. They are currently aiming to eradicate maternal and neonatal tetanus globally by 2005, through an immunisation programme in low-income countries. And they need volunteers to help them. But the volunteers will not be administering the vaccine, or working overseas to coordinate the programme. UNICEF needs volunteers to raise money in the UK. So the front line work is abroad, and the volunteers are in a (vital) support role. So how might UNICEF link the work of volunteers in this country with the need they meet abroad?

Awareness = 25 new-born babies, and 4 mothers, die every hour from tetanus.

Interest = UNICEF is vaccinating mothers to protect them and their unborn child from a needless death. It costs £1 to vaccinate each woman. UNICEF volunteers raise money through street collections, local appeals and fundraising events (such as coffee mornings and fêtes) to pay for vaccinations. With their help, UNICEF plans to eradicate maternal and neo-natal tetanus globally by 2005.

In this example (which we've drafted from information provided on UNICEF's website) potential volunteers can see how the work done in this country makes a difference abroad.

A word about using statistics

Statistics can be an effective way of illustrating the size of a problem if they are used sparingly. Statistics in themselves are not inherently interesting. They are only as powerful as the ability of people to comprehend them, and big numbers presented out of context can say very little. It is only when the audience can compare the statistics to something meaningful that they will have an impact. In the UNICEF example, the number of new-born babies dying from tetanus every year is 200,000. This is largely meaningless to most of us. However, when the statistics are presented as 25 deaths an hour, it is easier to understand the scale of the problem. Similarly, giving the cost of vaccination per person has much more impact than the cost of a whole vaccination programme. It also means that volunteers know the difference they make by each pound they raise.

As a rule of thumb avoid using statistics unless you can break them down into a comprehensible size, and relate them to the work that volunteers do.

Desire

What can your organisation offer that will make volunteering with you attractive?

Everyone who chooses to volunteer is motivated to do so for a range of reasons, and in one way or another they want it to be a satisfying and rewarding experience. This part of the recruitment message is your opportunity to 'sell' your voluntary work on its rewards. It is therefore helpful to flag up the ways in which a particular volunteer role will fulfil people. By doing so you can make your work more attractive and desirable to people who are motivated in those ways.

Not many recruitment messages we've seen really talk about what is in it for the volunteers, other than perhaps training or expenses. This example from the Terrence Higgins Trust, however, stands out as one of the better examples:

'What will you get from being a Buddy? Being a Buddy can be very demanding but immensely rewarding. Everyone volunteering as a Buddy should get some personal benefits, regardless of previous work or life experience. For some it may be new skills gained from our training and the work they do as a Buddy, whilst for others it may be personal growth and development. Many Buddies tell us they get great satisfaction from knowing they have "given something back" to the community. Buddying can also be a way to meet new people, through your support group and other THT events.'

While there is sometimes a degree of altruism involved in someone's decision to volunteer, it is rarely the only thing that motivates them. Particularly when people have settled into doing their voluntary work, altruism alone will rarely keep them stimulated. And, increasingly, more people these days volunteer with a very clear idea of what they want to get out of the experience – perhaps skills development and training, or a way of filling spare time and meeting new people.

Conversely, those who won't be motivated by what the work has to offer will be discouraged from applying. This is a good thing (yes, really). By giving people enough information to select themselves out of the process, you avoid wasting time. If they are not going to enjoy volunteering with you, surely it is better that they make that decision from the outset rather than after you've spent your time (and theirs) going through selection, induction and training procedures.

Voluntary work such as fundraising, organising events, sports coaching and campaigning will often appeal to those who are achievement orientated or perhaps even competitive. On the other hand, roles such as shop workers, befrienders and buddies, hospital volunteers and drivers may appeal more to those who enjoy camaraderie and social interaction. People attracted to becoming trustees, advocates, lobbying volunteers, media workers and speakers are likely to be those who enjoy having a say and influencing outcomes.

These are general examples of the ways in which certain roles can be motivating, but you can be even more specific. The best way to find out why people enjoy volunteering with you is to ask those who are already doing it. Even if you think you know, or can guess, why certain roles are rewarding it is worth talking to your existing volunteers. You may be surprised at the answers you get. Gather as many views as you can and then pick out those most commonly expressed to use in your recruitment campaigns.

As well as mentioning the motivational rewards that the work offers, you can also talk about some of the other material benefits such as reimbursing of expenses, training, support for volunteers and the resources you make available to them. It is important to be clear, however, that these are not in themselves factors that motivate people, but they can help to reassure those who might be anxious about volunteering.

In some situations you may wish to use the AIDA formula in a different order, and start your message with the 'desire' element. If your volunteers receive valuable work experience or training, for example, you might want to lead with that element in a message to an audience of students or unemployed young people. Here the judgement you need to make is whether you believe your voluntary work is more likely to appeal to your audience's self-interest than to their altruism. If there are particularly strong benefits arising from your voluntary work then you can play to that strength and open your message with the 'desire' component. If, on the other hand, talking about the needs you address is more likely to grab people's attention, then retain the original order of AIDA. If all that sounds too complicated, perhaps you need to try out both approaches and see which one is more successful.

Action

The final part of your recruitment message should focus on the action you want people to take next. Do they phone you for an information pack, or make an appointment to see you? Do they need to fill out an application form?

Aim to make the next step as easy as possible for your new recruits. If your recruitment message has got them fired up to help you, you won't want to dampen their enthusiasm by making the next step too difficult or lengthy.

If you give out a phone number, make sure it is staffed at all times and has an answering machine for out-of-hours callers. If you send out information packs or applications, aim to turn around requests for them within 48 hours. We recently saw a recruitment message that promised to get information back to you within a month. A month!! What kind of message does that send to prospective volunteers about their importance and value in that organisation?

Consider, too, using information technology. If you are online, give out an e-mail address. And if your organisation has a website, devote a page to volunteering with full information about the roles available and an online application form. We looked at the websites of Britain's 10 biggest charities. Of those who involve volunteers (most of them) there was information online about volunteering. But it wasn't always easy to find. In some cases, it was buried deep within the website and in most cases, it wasn't possible to apply online.

Using the AIDA formula

You can use AIDA with all kinds of recruitment media, whether posters or leaflets, advertisements or press releases, websites, mailshots or talks and presentations. The only difference will be in how much you can say in each of the four stages. With a poster or advert it will be very brief indeed, whereas a leaflet or mailshot gives you much more room to expand on Awareness, Interest, Desire and Action.

Using AIDA in your recruitment

- Don't fall into the trap of talking from your organisation's point of view. Keep your message focussed on the needs of your clients or cause, and then move on to talk from the audience's perspective

- Don't be tempted to dumb down your message. Keep it sharp and specific. Many organisations produce recruitment materials that are bland or vague out of a fear that they will put people off if they say too much. If you require volunteers to commit a certain amount of time, or have particular skills, say so from the outset. The only people you will put off are those who don't meet your criteria. In which case you've lost nothing at all

- Think about your recruitment strategy. If you are clear on who you are trying to reach it will become more obvious which recruitment medium you should use. This way you can avoid mistakes such as producing a load of leaflets, only to discover that an ad reaches your audience best. Work it all out from the start in your recruitment plan

- Think about the location of your audience. This will also influence your choice of communication methods. If you are targeting people in the workplace, for example, you could give a presentation, put a poster up in the canteen, circulate an e-mail or place an ad in the staff bulletin. Or if you want to reach trained counsellors through a professional journal, the options include inserting a leaflet, placing an ad, writing to the letters page and sending them a press release

- Balance time and cost against the impact of your means of communication. Clearly, you want to make the biggest and best impression possible, but limits on your budget and time may restrict your choices. That full colour glossy brochure is just never going to happen. But by examining your recruitment budget and work plan you will more easily be able to see which options are affordable. You do have a work plan by now, don't you?

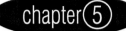

chapter (5)

KEEP IT UP

What are you having for dinner tonight? If you're like millions of other people in this country you will probably dig around in your fridge or freezer to see what you've got in. Shopping for groceries is one area of home life where we've learned to plan ahead, and we've turned food shopping into a major project that occurs once every week or two. It wasn't always this way and even today, some people continue to shop on a daily basis – getting only what is needed for today's meals.

The trouble with the weekly shop is that it can be hard to motivate yourself to go down to the supermarket, fight the crowds and load up the trolley. It becomes a major chore. By waiting until the fridge is empty we turn it into an urgent trip that we must make, regardless of whether it is a convenient time for us.

The daily shop, though, has lots to commend it. You only need to plan for one day at a time. You won't overstock on food you don't need. And food is fresher because it hasn't been slowly wilting away in your kitchen for a week. Unfortunately, shopping every day can be hard to fit in around all your other commitments. To make it work you may have to give up another activity.

Recruiting regularly

While we may not have persuaded you to give up your weekly trip to the supermarket, we would like to discourage you from using the same approach to finding new volunteers. Too often volunteer coordinators wait until they are short of help before looking for more. This not only turns recruitment into a crisis, but it burdens the recruitment drive with the need to deliver quickly. It forces recruitment to the top of the agenda regardless of what other work is in hand. If other work activities also need to be dealt with urgently then it's going to be a stressful few weeks trying to juggle them with the recruitment campaign. Who needs this kind of pressure?

So the key to recruitment is a little and often. The daily shop. Keep recruitment in front of you on a day-to-day basis with a rolling programme of campaigns that you are constantly keeping fresh. Instead of having to generate large numbers of applicants in one go, you can be satisfied with a small but steady supply.

The other big benefit of day-to-day recruitment is that it means that the public is constantly being exposed to your ads and publicity materials. You'll always have some campaign or other on the go, reaching people with your message about volunteering. This is advantageous because people don't always respond to your recruitment campaign immediately. Someone seeing your appeal for volunteers might well be interested, but may want to leave it until a more suitable time – after their holiday, say, or when the kids start school. If, by then, your recruitment messages are no longer in circulation, how will they be reminded to apply? Where will they find your contact details when they need them?

As we saw in Chapter 4, a good deal of commercial advertising does not aim to tell us about the product – it is assumed we know that already. But repeated advertising aims to keep the product fresh in our minds, a constant reminder. In the voluntary sector we assume that the occasional hit-and-run recruitment strategy will attract enough potential volunteers within the short space of time it is in circulation. In fact, you'd have to be an advertising genius to make that strategy work.

Making day-to-day recruitment work

So the daily shop has much to commend it in relation to finding volunteers. However, it does have some drawbacks.

Time lags between recruitment and training

There can be a problem concerning the need to synchronise the arrival of new volunteers with your training and induction programme. This is chiefly an issue for those organisations whose volunteers attend a series of training events before being eligible to begin their voluntary work. Large-scale training of this sort may be run only two or three times a year, so volunteers may be expected to wait several months between the time they apply and the start of their training. It can be hard for them to sustain their interest and motivation during the wait, and some volunteers will inevitably find something else to do instead.

For this reason it may be tempting to stick with having a short burst of recruitment in the weeks leading up to each training season. Yet many people tell us that they just can't make this work effectively – volunteers simply don't come running the minute you snap your fingers. Opportunities for volunteering need to be available at times which suit the people applying, not just your organisation.

To help you orchestrate the arrival of new volunteers with scheduled training events you could increase the frequency of your induction programme. Doing so will mean that volunteers don't have as much opportunity to lose momentum between application and training.

The obvious disadvantage of this is the increase in time and expense incurred. Some organisations get around this by sharing their training programme with other similar groups locally. By identifying where there is a cross-over in, say, core skills training, they have designed a workshop together which they either take turns to run or deliver jointly. Each organisation will still hold a short induction for their own volunteers dealing with issues specific to them, but this is much less time consuming. Joint training is not only a great example of organisations working cooperatively for mutual benefit but it also allows resources to be pooled for more efficient use – while intakes of new volunteers can occur more frequently.

If it is not possible to run your induction training more often then you could find other ways of utilising new volunteers while they wait for the next course to take place. This might involve finding work that they could do in a support or administrative role, which would give them the opportunity to get to know the organisation better while sustaining their motivation.

Too many volunteers

Another problem that can arise from day-to-day recruitment is that you end up with too many volunteers. While this is a nice predicament to be in, it is nonetheless a problem, and one most likely to be experienced by smaller organisations. As most projects don't accept just anybody as a volunteer, you may simply have to choose the best of the bunch and say 'no' to the others. If you've made it clear to potential volunteers that you have a selection process – and criteria they need to measure up to – they will understand that acceptance is not automatic. This may challenge some people's perception that volunteers can do what they like but it wouldn't do any harm to kill off that myth.

If, however, you find it's just too heartbreaking to turn away good people, then you have a real opportunity to rethink how you could expand the role of volunteers to help your organisation meet its aims. Consider delivering new services or improving support to existing staff and volunteers. And if that's not possible, why not network with other organisations in your area that offer similar voluntary work and refer your surplus onto them. Your local volunteer bureau will also be able to pass volunteers on (see *Useful Addresses* for contact details).

Finding the time to recruit

The final problem you will need to confront with day-to-day recruitment is finding the time to do it. Like the daily shop, it can be difficult to fit recruitment around other priorities and responsibilities. And yet it is vital to find a way of doing this. Recruitment is often unsuccessful simply because it is not undertaken regularly enough.

Organisations seem much better at finding the time for fundraising. They have to be. Failure to generate enough income threatens everything they do. So the fundraisers are getting on with it on a daily basis. You need to take the same approach with generating new volunteers. You will only be successful if you build it into the regular routine of your workload rather than treating it as an occasional special event. If that means reorganising the distribution of work then do it. And if you have nobody to whom you can delegate some of your tasks, well, recruit a volunteer. Make it part of your recruitment strategy to find new people to help you do some of the work that gets in the way of recruitment. Or find some volunteers who will organise the recruitment campaign for you.

Linking volunteer recruitment to PR

This book has discussed a number of proactive ways in which you can go out and find the volunteers you need. Yet, as you've probably experienced for yourself, not all volunteers are directly recruited by you. Sometimes they find you first.

This is great when it happens but we wouldn't call it a strategy. It relies on the spontaneous action of the volunteer while your role remains largely passive. Much of it is down to luck, so it would be foolhardy to rely on this mode of recruitment alone. Even when organisations receive a large number of unsolicited applications they will often find that only a small proportion come from people with the right skills and qualities.

Although you can't control spontaneous recruitment there are things you can do to influence it. When prospective volunteers take the initiative to contact you it often arises from your presence in the community, and the kind of profile you have in the media. Somehow or other they have heard about you, like what you do and want to know if they can be part of it. Every visible presence you have in the public eye has the potential to generate an interest in volunteering. In what way, then, can your organisation's public relations activity encourage spontaneous volunteering?

This may be a question that is new to you. In fact, many organisations don't associate PR with volunteer recruitment at all, and this can be a real missed opportunity.

PR tips that will support your recruitment activity

- Include a section on volunteering in all your organisation's publicity materials – leaflets, brochures, displays, website, videos and so on. Make sure your annual report mentions the ways in which volunteers have contributed to your organisation's work in the previous year
- When your colleagues undertake speaking engagements or attend public events encourage them to talk about the work of your volunteers
- Brief your volunteers so that they can speak knowledgeably about your organisation
- Continually take photographs of your volunteers in action to include in publicity materials, annual reports, newsletters and press releases
- Build up a good relationship with your local press, send them regular press releases and invite them to attend special events
- Mark the start or completion of particular volunteering projects by holding a special event. Give out volunteer awards to those who have completed a significant term of service, or have achieved other distinctions
- Organise an open day so that people can come and find out more about your organisation and your volunteering programme
- Publish a newsletter to keep people informed and interested in your organisation and the work your volunteers do – post it on your website or circulate copies by e-mail.

If your organisation is not engaged in any PR work, you may be putting additional strain on your recruitment campaign. If people have heard your organisation's name and understand your aims then it only takes one step to prompt them into becoming more involved. If, however, your target audience has never heard about you then your recruitment message involves two steps – building familiarity with your organisation, and explaining what volunteering involves. The more work your recruitment message has to do, the harder it will be to get the results you want. If you can build familiarity in the public's mind through PR then your recruitment will be a step ahead.

Of course PR is not simply a lead-in to volunteer recruitment. It has wider benefits that will link to the strategy of your whole organisation. It lays the foundation for gaining the interest and goodwill of many different stakeholders – from clients and service-users, to funders and donors, and even prospective employees. Somebody in your organisation should be thinking about your profile and how it links to your strategies for service provision, fundraising, personnel, volunteering and so on. If you have no PR strategy in place it's not just volunteer recruitment that could suffer. If you want to read more about undertaking good PR, we recommend *The DIY Guide to Public Relations* by Moi Ali (see *Further Reading*).

In the early 1990s Fraser set up a volunteer programme for an ethical investment society that was a client of his at the time. The organisation was established on a not-for-profit basis to provide a source of finance for small businesses in developing countries. Investors in this country knew they wouldn't make a lot of money on their investment but that it would at least hold its value over time and, in the process, help people in need to work their way out of poverty. The scheme was designed to appeal to individuals with a strong social conscience who were looking for a more ethical means of financial investment.

After the society had been established for a short time, it was decided that a volunteer programme would be set up. The volunteers' role would be to promote the society locally by giving talks, distributing publicity and so on. Yet the concept of the society's purpose was difficult to explain concisely. Fraser's initial approach, therefore, was to recruit within the society's membership, where people already understood the purpose of the organisation and could more easily grasp why volunteering was important. This produced a small core of committed volunteers but not enough to help the society achieve its investment targets.

The next step was to build recruitment on the back of the society's PR exposure. Wherever people learned about the society's existence a follow up with a recruitment message would be made. Unfortunately, the PR strategy ground to a halt. Other, more pressing, matters had pushed it down the agenda and at a time when the recruitment plan needed to follow up new contacts, there weren't any being made. It wasn't just the PR strategy that didn't get off the ground – neither did the recruitment campaign.

Responding to spontaneous applications

Regardless of how much you are able to influence your organisation's PR you are still likely to receive, one way or another, unsolicited enquiries about volunteering. Many of these people won't convert into active volunteers. Some won't have the skills or availability necessary for the work you need doing, while others will lose interest when they find out the nature of the voluntary work. There is a good possibility, though, that some will become reliable and effective volunteers for you. If you want to capitalise on this source of volunteers then you need to be geared up for their enquiries.

A volunteer who has responded to your recruitment campaign is probably applying to fill a specific role. Someone who volunteers spontaneously, however, may not know what roles are available. It is worthwhile preparing a summary of the different types of voluntary work within your organisation to give to enquirers. This might include a brief summary of the information included in all the role descriptions you hold. Try not to overload people with too much information, but give them enough to help them make some choices. Tell them about the kind of people you are looking for in terms of qualities, skills and the time commitment required. If you have a website you can always upload full role descriptions and person specifications onto it for people who want further information – or they can call you to find out more about a particular role that takes their interest.

Be flexible

From time to time people will offer you their professional skills. 'I'm a photographer and would be happy to do some work free of charge.' These kinds of proposals can be extremely useful. For one thing the offer of a specific service can prompt you to think about how you could use it, and that might help you to identify new and useful ways of involving volunteers. While it may not have crossed your mind to recruit, for example, a volunteer photographer, once you have one available it might really inspire you to find ways of utilising their skill.

In order to be able to make the most of these offers, you won't want to appear too inflexible. As well as giving out information about the standard volunteering roles available don't be afraid to ask people what they can do, or if they have a particular skill that might be useful. You might just find yourself hastily writing a role description and tailoring a brand new role around the offer of a specific individual.

Of course you still need to be certain that the new role is going to be both useful for your organisation and that the volunteer will be motivated enough to commit to it. Don't fall into the trap of creating roles for people merely because they don't want to do anything else. All of your volunteers should contribute to meeting your organisation's aims above all else. But if you let yourself be open to new possibilities you will probably discover some exciting new ways of involving volunteers.

George was a retired industrial chemist and lecturer who volunteered at Greenpeace. Originally his job was to reply to requests from the public for information about environmental issues. When he heard that one of the campaign teams was conducting research into a major chemical manufacturer that was polluting an important river, he offered to help. Not only was he able to access academic libraries for data about particular chemicals, but he had once worked for the manufacturer concerned. No one had ever thought of trying to recruit a volunteer with his insight and access to information – after all it would be so unlikely to succeed. But when George offered his services a role was created that would utilise his specialist skills and knowledge fully.

Other ways people can help you

As we mentioned earlier, many people who volunteer on their own initiative won't be suitable for – or have an interest in – the voluntary work you have available. But given the interest they have in your organisation, it would be a pity to lose their support completely. If it becomes clear that they are not going to be a volunteer, you might let them know about other ways in which they can be involved. Perhaps they could support you financially, or do some campaigning or letter writing for you? Maybe they could put a poster or a collecting tin in their place of work? Don't let a warm contact grow cold. Think about alternative ways that they can support your work.

MAKING YOUR ORGANISATION ATTRACTIVE TO VOLUNTEERS

In North London there's a lovely little pub called The Prince of Wales. It is an old traditional pub that has resisted being renovated in a faux antique style. It doesn't need to. The original gas lamps are still above the fireplace and fitted wooden benches run along the walls. You can get a great pint of bitter there and they usually have a guest ale or two on tap. It's a warm and cosy kind of place, where neither loud music nor a rowdy crowd will drown out your conversation. And, most surprisingly, they serve the most fantastic Thai food instead of traditional bar meals.

Pubs exist to serve drinks – it is their *raison d'être*. In that respect, arguably, they don't differ that much from each other. What makes a particular pub special are the other factors which combine to draw you towards it – its location, the friendliness of the staff, the atmosphere, the other customers, the food and so on.

When volunteers come to your organisation it is not simply the work that will make it an enjoyable experience. The support you offer, the friendliness and enthusiasm of people, the appreciation shown, the fact that expenses are reimbursed and an attractive environment are among the many factors that can make volunteering fun. Creating a welcoming and supportive setting for volunteers plays an important part in drawing them towards you. And in the same way you would not be attracted to an unwelcoming pub, volunteers may have anxieties about working with you that discourage them from stepping inside. If your recruitment campaign is going to be successful, you will need to check you've removed some of the obstacles that can put volunteers off.

Demonstrate that you are well organised

One guaranteed disincentive to people is volunteer management which is haphazard, uncoordinated and unsystematic. If people are going to commit their time to you they want to know that you will make the best use of it. They don't want to feel like an afterthought, or even a nuisance, because you are too busy doing other things to give them the support they need.

Respond promptly and efficiently

When someone requests information about volunteering, deal with it promptly. Have an information pack or leaflet available which clearly spells out what being a volunteer involves and the steps it takes to become one. Aim to mail it out within 48 hours of receiving the request. By responding promptly you are sending out a strong non-verbal message to the prospective volunteer that they are important to you, that you are well organised and keen to have their support. Your actions send a more powerful and believable message about the importance of volunteers than anything you could ever say in a leaflet.

Your first contact with prospective volunteers on the phone should be equally efficient and well organised. In an article in *The Journal of Volunteer Administration* (see *Further Reading*), Charles J. Hobson and Kathryn L. Malec offer some guidelines on making that first conversation count.

Key quality indicators in initial telephone contact with prospective volunteers

1. Answer the phone within three rings
2. Provide a greeting
3. Provide the name of the organisation
4. Offer assistance to the caller
5. Provide the name of the person answering the call
6. Use the caller's name in the conversation
7. Ask for the caller's full name and telephone number so you can call them back
8. If you need to call them back, be sure to follow through and make the call
9. Do not ask a prospective volunteer to call the organisation back
10. Extend an invitation to visit the organisation
11. Inquire about the caller's skills
12. Ask the caller about the number of hours they have available to give
13. Ask the caller if references can be arranged
14. If the caller's skills are incompatible with the organisation's needs, refer them to another organisation
15. Thank the person for calling.

Of course it is equally possible that prospective volunteers may contact you by e-mail. An electronic message carries with it an expectation of a prompt reply because the sender knows you will receive it as soon as you log on to your computer. A reply sent by return is not only courteous but tells the enquirer that you value their interest in volunteering and take them seriously.

Delivering this standard of service may require some rethinking about your systems and procedures. It can be helpful to log all enquiries about volunteering so that you know when a request was made and the means of communication (post, phone, e-mail, in person). You can then easily check that you are responding swiftly enough to requests for information. Incidentally, you can also use your log to review the volume of enquiries you get, calculate what proportion convert to actual volunteers and what the most popular means of communication is. You can then build this data into future strategies: how can you improve conversion rates, or better respond to enquiries by whatever means most potential volunteers use?

Making a good impression face to face

If you recruit volunteers by giving talks, or setting up a recruitment stand, you have other opportunities to demonstrate how well organised you are:

- Make sure you show up on time and have all the resources you need to hand.
- Plan your verbal recruitment message so that you are clear and succinct.
- Think too about how you will follow up any enquirers you meet. Make a point of learning enquirers' names, and using them in conversation.
- Try to have some written information available about volunteering for your organisation – a well-produced leaflet suggests that volunteers are integral to your organisation rather than an afterthought. And writing it will help you think through your recruitment message.

If you arrange for volunteers to meet you for an exploratory chat, be ready to greet them and don't keep them waiting. If you have a reception desk, brief the staff so that they can be welcoming. Prepare some other colleagues and volunteers so that when you introduce them to the visitor, they can use the person's name. Arrange a meeting room where you won't be distracted, and have a clear structure for your discussion (which you might outline to the volunteer at the start).

By showing that you have prepared for the volunteer's visit you make it clear how important they are to your organisation.

Addressing common anxieties about volunteering

If people are unfamiliar with your work or your client group they may have anxieties about volunteering with you. These can range from fears about their safety to concerns about their competence to do the work well.

Safety fears can revolve around a number of issues. Are volunteers expected to work with a client group they think could be dangerous? Will they feel worried about travelling to, or working in, your neighbourhood? Are they going to have to work with machinery or equipment that is potentially dangerous?

Whether you consider these fears realistic or not, you need to take them seriously. Even if – or perhaps especially if – people's concerns are borne out of ignorance or prejudice you need to tackle them. Don't be tempted to make judgements about their concerns or merely dismiss them as silly. From the volunteer's point of view there is a good reason why such fears exist. By helping people to overcome their anxieties about personal safety you are maximising your outreach to potential volunteers.

Similarly, there are good reasons why potential volunteers might have concerns about their competence. Fear of failure can often deter people from trying something new. This is so common, in fact, that those who don't allow fear of failure to hold them back are often widely admired. (In March 2002 a poll of public relations experts voted Sir Richard Branson one of the most effective PR campaigners. This was attributed, in part, to his 'At least I tried' philosophy. The panel said, 'Any business disappointments or personal failures seem to endear him to the public further'.)

For the rest of us, however, concerns about embarrassing ourselves or letting others down can be enough to hold us back. Prospective volunteers may feel they lack the skills, experience or qualifications to serve you well, and they worry about coping with the work, damaging your organisation or disappointing your staff or clients. They might even feel that they need to have a certain status to undertake your voluntary work, and that to apply would be 'pushing themselves forward' arrogantly.

One of the difficulties about countering people's fears is that you first need to know what they are. Your existing volunteers may be of limited help here. You could assume that, as they already work with you, they either overcame their anxieties or didn't have them in the first place. On the other hand, as they are most familiar with the voluntary work, they may have some useful insights into what may concern people. If you decide to involve your current volunteers in identifying fears, it is probably worth balancing their views with those of people outside your organisation. Try and poll a diverse group of people by presenting them with information about your voluntary work: the service-users, location and times of work, the particular responsibilities of each role, commitment required and so on. Ask what concerns they might have about volunteering with you, then prioritise your results.

With this kind of information you can work towards reducing common fears. You can use your recruitment messages or information packs either to challenge wrong assumptions, or to reassure potential volunteers about the steps you take to minimise actual risks.

Jo works for a mental health charity. She looks for volunteers to work with adults who have mental health problems. The volunteers befriend clients on a one-to-one basis. She has learned that prospective volunteers have a number of concerns about this type of work: will they be at risk from physical attack, will they be able to cope with behaviour they find challenging, might they have to handle emergency situations where a client has, say, harmed themselves?

She decided to try to alleviate these concerns by including the following points in the organisation's recruitment literature:

- You will not work with patients who have just left hospital or have a history of violence
- All clients are screened by a Community Psychiatric Nurse
- You do not need to have any prior knowledge about mental health issues
- We will train and match you carefully with an appropriate client
- You will be supported by an experienced volunteer coordinator and have easy access to a range of specialists.

Additional ways of addressing potential volunteers' concerns include:

- inviting them to come for a day to see what the work involves and to talk to current volunteers, staff and clients;
- quoting, in your recruitment messages, existing volunteers' accounts of how easily they have adjusted to volunteering, how they cope and how well supported they feel;
- starting new volunteers in an 'easy' role then moving them into more responsible work when they feel comfortable with it.

Run a well-resourced volunteer programme

If your volunteer programme is badly funded it will be difficult to attract people to it. Most volunteers want to be able to do their work well and not face constant hurdles created by a lack of the necessary resources, equipment or staff time. There are some essential funding issues that need to be addressed here, and they challenge a widely believed myth – that volunteers are free.

Volunteers are anything but free. They are not even cheap, and if your organisation is serious about involving them effectively, you need to allocate adequate funding to them. If you are the type of organisation that is mostly (or entirely) run by volunteers you will need to ensure your fundraising strategy includes covering costs for volunteer involvement – encompassing everything from travel expenses and meals, to equipment and materials, recruitment and training, and insurance. If you are an organisation that is largely run by employees then your senior management team will need to allocate a sufficient budget to the volunteer programme.

If you are not taking volunteers seriously in your financial provision how can you expect them to be committed to giving their time to you? Too many organisations abuse the goodwill of volunteers by claiming they don't have the money to fund the programme better. In fact what this often *really* means is that they haven't bothered to find the money, or they have made a choice to allocate it to other areas of work they deem more important. In either case the message is clear: volunteers are not worth making a financial commitment to. It won't take people long to see through that attitude and express their opinion with their feet.

Paying expenses

Probably the biggest chunk of money you need to allocate to volunteers is in covering their expenses. It is now common practice for organisations to pay (up to a clearly defined limit) the costs that volunteers incur in the course of their volunteering. Typically this might include travel, meals, and other direct costs related to volunteering (telephone calls, postage and so on). In some cases – though this is still relatively rare – costs towards childcare are reimbursed (or the organisation arranges its own childminding facilities).

It is now considered best practice to insist that volunteers claim expenses, rather than to offer them the choice. This move is largely driven by equal opportunities, where procedures should be standardised to avoid excluding those on low incomes. If some volunteers don't claim their expenses it can be awkward and embarrassing for those who really need to, and disadvantageous to the organisation. We've heard some volunteers volubly express the view that they think it is wrong to claim expenses, and who have said so in front of people who are so financially hard pressed that they couldn't volunteer without reimbursement. Think about the chair of the committee who pays a lot out of her own pocket for the refreshments at meetings, as well as for her phone calls and petrol costs, and little gifts for volunteers' birthdays. Would a person on a low income be encouraged to take over this role if they presumed they would have to do the same?

Volunteers can always discreetly donate their expenses back to the organisation at a later date. But by having claimed them in the first place they will have helped to create a climate where receiving expenses is the norm, and you will have a much clearer idea about the true cost of volunteer involvement.

Equipment and materials

Making sure that volunteers have the equipment and materials necessary to do their job will also help to make volunteering with you more appealing – particularly if such resources are of good quality and not just the cast-offs from employees.

Where volunteers are office based try to create an attractive environment that is clean and appealingly decorated. Ensure that volunteers have a sense of ownership in their work space, such as a regular desk that they can use with their own drawer or in-tray, and an ample supply of stationery. We've witnessed, more than once, organisations recruiting volunteers even although there is nowhere for them to sit and work. So plan it well from the outset and consider the resource implications of bringing in each new volunteer.

For those volunteering roles where specific equipment is needed – such as catering, gardening or decorating – make sure the tools are up to the job. Do the can-openers work, are the shears sharp, and do the paintbrushes have bristles? Is there a piece of equipment – a food processor, wheelbarrow or paint roller – that would make life easier for volunteers? If your volunteers are bringing in their own gear, take the hint.

Training

Of course you might want to train volunteers in how to look after the equipment they use so that it lasts longer. Any training you provide presents a good opportunity to help volunteers do the best job possible. But consider too the way in which the training you offer can be an incentive to volunteer. Many people are attracted to volunteering because of the opportunity to learn new skills, so use this as an inducement in your recruitment campaigns.

Training can take the form of workshops, conferences, on-the-job coaching, peer group review, learning cells, videos, or reading books, journals and manuals. Your existing staff and volunteers already have a considerable amount of expertise that they can pass on. Many organisations underestimate the amount of knowledge and experience they already possess, and the capacity they have to shape it into attractive and useful training programmes. Do you?

Remember, your volunteers will gossip

If your volunteers really enjoy what they are doing they will tell others about it. If they hate what they are doing, well, they will tell others about that too. Your existing volunteers can either be your greatest ambassadors or your biggest critics. One way or another, they will help to create locally the image of your volunteer programme. If you work at giving them a rewarding and satisfying experience they will help to attract new people as volunteers.

Make volunteering rewarding

Volunteers want to be part of an organisation where people love the work they do, are good at it, know that they are making a difference, feel their contribution is recognised, and understand they have the opportunity to develop in the job or focus on what they like doing best.

Creating this kind of work environment takes time. It requires continuous attention to make volunteering rewarding and exciting. It starts by making sure volunteers get a sense of achievement from the work they are doing. Through coaching and supervision, you can equip them with the skills and knowledge they need to do the job well. It will also help if each volunteer is matched to a role in which they are most likely to succeed.

Providing feedback and recognition also contributes to sustaining volunteers' enthusiasm. Finding ways to measure the outcome of their work will help everyone to understand clearly the difference they are making, as well as prompt them to think about how they could be more effective. Volunteers are more likely to feel recognised and appreciated if they receive regular updates on the impact of their work on your services or cause. And, of course, regular thanks and appreciation, demonstrated in a variety of ways by a range of different people, count for a lot. Take the time to make people feel good about their volunteering and they will tell their friends about it.

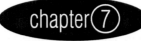

DIVERSIFYING YOUR VOLUNTEERS

Imagine you are the managing director of a theatre. You're worried that your audience is too middle aged and middle class and you want to attract younger people. What do you do? Perhaps you could focus your advertising on media that younger people favour. After all, if you make them more aware of what you have to offer, surely more of them will come along?

Your marketing manager, however, decides to conduct some research by going out and talking to younger people. The results of the survey show that young people think your plays are boring, the auditorium is too cramped, the tickets are over-priced and that the drinks in your bar are too old-fashioned. You begin to realise that diversifying your audience is going to involve more than just altering your advertising strategy – some major changes to the way your theatre is run and to your facilities are called for.

Why diversify your volunteers?

You can't successfully improve the variety of your volunteers without examining seriously all aspects of your organisation. Paying lip service to diversity in order to appear politically correct will not get you anywhere. But widening the range of your volunteers requires commitment, time, effort and expense. And you will need to be able to justify this within your organisation. It is similar to giving up smoking – unless you're convinced that the benefits outweigh the struggle to change, you will not succeed.

Different organisations have their own reasons for wanting to attract a wider variety of volunteers. For some, the quest for better diversity aims to produce volunteers who are more representative of the community in which they operate or relevant to the services they provide. How can a team of white staff and volunteers successfully deliver neighbourhood services to a largely West African community?

In other cases certain types of volunteers may bring a particular quality to your volunteer programme. People over fifty, for example, are more likely to serve for longer than younger volunteers who relocate more frequently.

And then there are plenty of organisations who actively want to support the values behind equal opportunities by attracting volunteers who may be disadvantaged in society – asylum seekers, one-parent families, offenders or people with physical and/or learning difficulties.

Attracting a diverse range of volunteers provides your organisation with a great opportunity to learn and improve understanding between genders, cultures and generations. If your project exists to improve some aspect of society, how can you be successful if people from a range of backgrounds are not taking an active part in your work?

Setting specific targets

It is difficult to improve diversity without clearly setting out to attract those sectors of society that are under-represented in your volunteer programme. It is not simply a matter of saying 'we accept anyone'. You need to be proactive in reaching out to particular communities. Different target groups have their own set of needs and require different approaches.

If you want to attract younger volunteers, who do you mean by younger – 16–20 year olds? 25–35 year olds? 50–60 year olds? If you say you want to attract more Asian people what communities and nationalities are you referring to? If you need more disabled volunteers, which disability is your priority? Visual impairment, deafness, physical and learning disabilities – each of these requires a different strategy for recruitment and support.

It is best to assess the diversity of your current volunteers before working out how to recruit those who are under-represented. The categories listed in the box opposite will give you some insight into what diversity means but we're sure that you can think of more which are relevant to your situation.

Unless you are working in a large organisation with hundreds of volunteers you will probably already have a rough idea of the composition of your volunteer force without doing a survey. However, some categories may not be clearly evident to you (such as volunteers' mental health history, some disabilities, sexuality, family status etc.) and so an anonymous survey may be useful even within a small project.

Armed with this knowledge you can determine whether or not you feel the composition of your volunteers is properly representative or appropriate. One way of doing this is to compare your volunteers with the population in your catchment area. Information and statistics are available on the internet (for example, www.statistics.gov.uk) or from your local council.

Diversity of volunteers – categories to consider

- Age
- Gender
- Sexual orientation
- Cultural background
- Ethnic origin
- Income level
- Professional skills, academic or vocational qualifications
- Family status: single, married, with or without children
- Physical disability
- Learning difficulty
- Mental illness or previous mental illness
- Accents
- Immigration status
- Rehabilitated drug abusers
- Employed/unemployed
- Geographical area (living and working)
- Extrovert/introvert
- Political affiliation
- Persons with spent or unspent convictions.

Another criterion you can use to evaluate your current diversity against is the purpose, or aim, of your organisation. If, for example, your *raison d'être* is to empower disabled people then it would be sensible if a large proportion of your volunteers has a disability.

Once you have assessed your current diversity you can then prioritise which members of the community you want to target. Define some recruitment goals which clearly identify who you are aiming to attract: 'By the end of April we will have recruited eight volunteers, both male and female, from the Pakistani community who will work with disabled children from Pakistani and other backgrounds'.

Overcoming obstacles to volunteering

People from some sections of the community may have reservations about volunteering with you. Whether through concerns they have, such as fear of discrimination, or practical barriers such as accessibility, their anxieties are worth hearing and responding to. By talking directly to the kind of people you want to recruit, but who have so far failed to volunteer, you can find out what discourages their involvement. Understanding the barriers they face is as important as demonstrating the potential opportunities you can offer to them. Only by finding ways of removing these obstacles will the opportunities for volunteering be available to them.

Below we explore five particular sectors of society, look at the issues that face them in relation to volunteering, and suggest practical ways of reaching out to them.

People with a physical disability, learning disability or a mental health problem

People with a disability still feel that many organisations exclude them as volunteers because of a lack of awareness about their existence, the skills they have to offer or through long-standing prejudices against them. In some cases concerns about the cost of providing extra support to disabled volunteers, or adapting the premises, can prevent organisations from encouraging disabled people to volunteer. We have even worked with disability organisations that have no disabled volunteers working for them.

If you want to attract volunteers with disabilities you need to be very explicit in demonstrating your desire to recruit them. Find out where you can reach them locally, such as independent living centres, special schools, social services or health centres, other specialist organisations and clubs, internet groups and websites, and so on. Consult with people who have disabilities about the kinds of voluntary roles that would appeal to them, or how existing roles could be adjusted to meet their needs.

If your premises are inaccessible to disabled volunteers – and there is no prospect of adapting them – identify roles that can be fulfilled from home. These could include giving advice over the telephone or by e-mail, undertaking research, editing newsletters or updating websites.

Organise disability awareness training for everyone in your organisation. Consider making your recruitment materials available in braille, large print, floppy disk, CD-ROM or audiotape. Make it clear in your recruitment messages that you welcome volunteers with special needs or disabilities.

If you have little experience of working with disabled people, you may not feel confident about thinking through all the relevant issues yourself. It can therefore be extremely useful to collaborate with local disability organisations – ask for their advice on different types of disabilities, how to support volunteers who have them and where you can go to recruit them.

Young people (16–25 year olds)

The early 1990s saw a downturn in the number of young people volunteering and there have been a number of initiatives in recent times to try and reverse this tendency. Only when the results of the next survey of volunteering trends are published will we know how successful these have been, but schemes such as Millennium Volunteers are expected to have played a key role in re-engaging young people in voluntary work.

We can only hope that this is the case. The involvement of young people in volunteering is precious, not only for the energy and new perspectives they bring, but also because it paves the way for the future of the voluntary sector. People who have rewarding and satisfying volunteering experiences in their youth are more likely to continue with voluntary work in later life, and for some it will be a preparation for a career in the sector. We treat youth volunteering lightly at our own risk.

Hopefully, the success of new schemes to promote volunteering among young people will help to remove some of the obstacles that historically have discouraged them. Volunteering has not always had a good image among the young, and continues to be perceived by many as boring and dominated by white, well-to-do, middle-aged women. Perhaps we've only ourselves to blame for this lingering outdated stereotype. Many young people remain unaware of the opportunities for volunteering that are available to them, and the personal benefits arising from them.

While some positive PR among young people wouldn't do the voluntary sector any harm, it won't, by itself, engage their interest in volunteering. Even those who are willing to volunteer face a range of obstacles. Volunteering can cost money – even where expenses are reimbursed, you still need to spend money before you can claim it back. Some voluntary work is inaccessible if you don't have your own transport, particularly in rural areas. And volunteering takes time, which can be a real problem for those who are studying – especially near exam times. And if they manage to overcome all of those hurdles, what happens when young volunteers turn up only to discover that the work is badly organised and uninteresting?

If you're serious about attracting younger people, you will need to give some careful thought to the kind of roles you offer them and the way the voluntary work is organised.

Above all, volunteering must be enjoyable. Young people want to get involved in activities that are not only fun but focus on issues relevant to them and their concerns. Projects centred on bullying, the environment, sports, campaign work, disadvantaged children and so on are particularly attractive. Try and offer voluntary work that can be done with friends or in groups, where there is some degree of self-direction. The more opportunity there is for young people to put their own ideas into action, and to influence the work they do, the more motivated and committed they are likely to be. Try to delegate as much control and choice as you reasonably can.

Remember, too, that those who are at school or university have their year organised into bite-sized chunks, and that their availability during term time will differ from the holidays. Aim to offer projects that have a fixed length and end time, and that give volunteers some sense of completion. Providing a certificate or reference at the end is also valued.

Keep the voluntary work varied and flexible by offering a wide range of tasks and activities. Young people often welcome challenging opportunities that allow them to exercise their existing talents as well as developing new skills, so when you are recruiting young volunteers make a point of selling the benefits to them. Explain the ways in which being a volunteer will support their personal development, and allow them to practise skills that are applicable in the workplace as well as enjoyable in their own right.

Clearly, all of this will require a good deal of support on your part, and you will need to think carefully about the training and supervision structures you put in place. If you currently have no young people volunteering, there may need to be quite a shake up, but once you get a few on board you can begin to encourage them to recruit others by word of mouth. It will also be easier for you to demonstrate the benefits of volunteering if you already have some examples of young people who have volunteered with you, and you can build their stories into presentations and talks for schools and colleges.

Ethnically diverse volunteers

Britain's multicultural society is not always well represented within many mainstream voluntary organisations and charities. That is not to say, however, that people from black, Asian and other minority ethnic communities don't volunteer. Indeed there is a very fine tradition of social involvement in many different cultures.

Given the rich variety of ethnic groups living in the UK we can't generalise too much about the issues raised by them in relation to volunteering. The traditions, outlooks and needs of one black community are not the same as those of every other one. On the other hand, this is not the place for a detailed exploration of voluntarism in each minority ethnic group, so we can only raise a few key points to think about.

If you wish to attract volunteers from other ethnic communities you firstly need to be aware that your audience of potential volunteers may already be active in their own community. This can include faith-based volunteering conducted through their place of worship. Don't assume that if people aren't volunteering with you they aren't volunteering at all. Your call on their time may be competing with existing voluntary commitments, but if you are not part of the same community, or faith, such volunteering may not be evident to you.

Other traditions of volunteering may also be more informal than the kind of volunteer programme you run. The moves that many of us have made towards more structured volunteer management in the last ten or fifteen years have played an important part in making volunteering more effective, satisfying and safe. However the increase in formal procedures can be perceived as overly bureaucratic by those more used to a communal style of volunteering. Consequently it may be more effective to recruit volunteers from some minority ethnic groups by word of mouth and networking, rather than through adverts and application forms.

To this end you might start by appointing trustees or management committee members from other ethnic communities. You could also take time to find out about community groups serving people of different ethnic backgrounds in your area, and explore building partnerships with them.

If you do decide to target recruitment ads at particular communities, be explicit about why you particularly welcome, for example, black volunteers and include comments from any who currently work with you. Even better, try to recruit a volunteer or employee from another ethnic group to orchestrate your recruitment activity.

Bear in mind, though, that potential volunteers from other ethnic groups may have reservations about joining you, fearing they will not be accepted or made to feel welcome. Those who have experienced racism in other fields of life may, understandably, prefer to continue volunteering within their own ethnic group. If you choose to reach out to them, are you certain that they won't experience discrimination in your organisation? Recognise and address institutional racism in your workplace by establishing effective policies and procedures, and by running cultural awareness and sensitivity training.

Older people

Many older people have discovered the benefits that volunteering can bring. Whether it is in helping to make the transition from work to retirement, providing an opportunity to utilise skills developed over the years, or as a way of retaining an active role in society, voluntary work has a lot to offer senior members of the community.

Unfortunately, many of these benefits are undermined by the way that some older people have been treated in the voluntary sector. While organisations can see the benefit of investing training and support in young people, they don't always view those in retirement in the same way. Older people are sometimes offered a limited choice of undemanding tasks, or are only given the opportunity to work with other older folk. And yet the skills and experience that they have to offer should make them among the most valued volunteers.

Like all volunteers, older people should be matched to a role that they are not only interested in but also have the skills and abilities to undertake adequately. The failure to do this has contributed towards some organisations having a poor opinion of older people – they put them into unsuitable roles and then complain they are ineffective.

If you want to attract older volunteers who can contribute successfully to your organisation, you will need to offer a rewarding experience in return. Provide opportunities to learn new skills and have interesting new experiences – don't presume everyone wants their personal development to stop when they reach 60. Develop roles that build upon their strengths, knowledge and life experience. Many organisations successfully engage older volunteers in the provision of services to young people, for instance as adopted grandparents to families in need, mentors to young students or young people at risk. For some reason, when you skip a generation there is often better mutual understanding than with the adjacent generation.

In your recruitment messages to older people, make a point of emphasising the benefits that your different volunteering roles offer. Make it clear that you reimburse expenses, and stress the comfort and accessibility of your premises if possible. Be aware that the language and terminology used in organisations today may be unfamiliar to those who have been out of the workplace for some time, so try to ensure that your recruitment materials are free of jargon.

If you provide training, some older people may be anxious about participating in it. You can help them to overcome their concerns by explaining why the training is important, what it will involve and how it will be of help to them. You might even consider using a 'softer' name for it such as information session, volunteer briefing or team discussion.

There are plenty of places frequented by older people where you can focus your recruitment activity – pensioners' clubs, church groups, community centres and so on. However, if you are seeking older people with particular skills, you might want to recruit via local employers – perhaps by contributing to pre-retirement courses. Some employers also have social clubs or newsletters to which retired employees continue to have access.

You could try approaching organisations such as REACH, which finds voluntary work for executives, and is an ideal way of finding someone with experience of a particular business skill. And at the time of writing the government has launched Experience Corps to encourage people over fifty to volunteer – you can find out how they can direct older volunteers to you by visiting their website (see *Useful Addresses*).

Lesbian, gay, bisexual or transgendered volunteers

Like most of the others groups we've mentioned in this chapter, lesbian, gay, bisexual or transgendered (LGBT) volunteers often focus their efforts on projects that address issues and concerns close to their hearts. Gay men, for example, undertake a considerable amount of work in HIV/AIDS services, safer sex education, and campaigning for gay rights.

But there are many LGBT volunteers in other fields of work. Consortium of Lesbian, Gay, Bisexual & Transgendered Voluntary and Community Organisations is a national membership organisation focusing on the development and support of LGB&T groups. It has a volunteer service which helps organisations promote volunteer roles to LGBT-registered volunteers. There are many LGBT volunteers who don't want to restrict their social involvement to the gay community but, like other minority groups, anxieties about how welcome and accepted they will be can be inhibiting.

By making a point of actively recruiting LGBT volunteers, you can override these concerns. By placing recruitment messages in lesbian and gay publications and venues you send a strong message of acceptance to these communities that you welcome their involvement and support.

The *Pink Paper* is a weekly gay and lesbian news magazine that is distributed nationally, and has appointments pages where you can place adverts for volunteers. The *Gay Times* is a monthly magazine (available from larger newsagents) that lists most of the gay clubs, bars and societies in the country. *Diva* is the equivalent publication for lesbian readers, also with full listings. Cafés are often a focus for information about community events and activities, where leaflets or posters can be displayed. You might also make contact with some of the support organisations and discussion groups in your area. There are now also an increasing number of festivals and gay pride events that take place around the country and you might consider tying in some recruitment activity with them.

Welcoming new volunteers

In many respects, your ability to embrace diversity hinges on how welcoming you are to new people. While others may be different from you in terms of age, gender, race or sexuality, anyone you meet for the first time is 'different' because they are unknown to you and unfamiliar. You may feel uncertain about how to relate to them.

In this sense, embracing diversity is about how willing you are to be open to new people and building relationships with them. Plenty of volunteers have felt unwelcome despite being the same colour, age and gender as the others around them. By learning to be more welcoming and accepting you cut across the obvious divides and see each new person as a unique individual in their own right.

> Julie was a volunteer at her local soup kitchen. When she arrived for her first day the other volunteers on the team were already busy going about their tasks and activities. The project coordinator kept Julie waiting for fifteen minutes while he sorted out some problems, and then put her to work chopping vegetables in a corner of the kitchen. At the end of the shift the volunteers sat down together for a cup of tea. For the first few minutes they talked to Julie and asked her some questions about herself, but quickly moved on to talk about a party they had all been to the previous weekend. How welcome and included do you think Julie felt?

Being welcoming is not merely a matter of being pleasant to people. To do it well, you need to make sure your behaviour, language, routine, thinking and attitudes are all geared towards welcoming the newcomer. This is relatively easy when you meet another person on a one-to-one basis, but considerably harder when you're introducing a new volunteer into your organisation. Here are some ways that you can encourage existing members of your organisation to welcome new people.

- Give each new volunteer a personal welcome to the organisation, and perhaps try to involve a senior manager or trustee in doing this.
- Make sure relevant people learn the names of new volunteers and make a point of introducing themselves.
- Introduce new volunteers at meetings, and consider using ice-breaker exercises as a way of helping people to get to know each other.
- Introduce a buddy system where an experienced volunteer links up with a new recruit.
- Adapt welcome packs and induction materials to the needs of different groups (language, font size, design and so on).
- Learn about special needs or customs, and adapt accordingly.
- Incorporate other cultures and traditions into the workplace – celebrate festivals or holidays, or vary music that is played or food served.
- Be aware of jokes and language that might be offensive.

- When you are introducing someone from a different group or community into your project make them aware they are pioneers and may still encounter some prejudices. Take time to review their experience and offer appropriate support.
- Consider how you might adapt meetings to the needs of new volunteers in terms of timing, style and location.
- Engage existing volunteers in discussions about diversity, and the benefits it brings to your organisation. Get them to reflect on what makes them feel welcome and consider how they can extend that to new volunteers.

chapter 8

USE YOUR IMAGINATION

It is easy to get stuck in a rut in the way you recruit volunteers. Organisations can easily fall into the trap of thinking that the only methods of finding volunteers are those they have traditionally used – regardless of whether they continue to be successful or not. Many recruiters also make the mistake of copying other organisations' recruitment tactics, again without necessarily knowing whether they work.

When we've run recruitment workshops we've found that participants are, not surprisingly, very keen to learn how others have succeeded in finding new volunteers. 'We placed an advert in the *Big Issue* and got loads of responses', one person will say. Meanwhile others in the group are furiously scribbling in their notebooks 'Place an ad in the *Big Issue*', the assumption being that if it worked for one organisation it will work for them. It's as if the recruitment method itself is imagined to carry some sort of talisman of success.

In fact, organisations that successfully recruit through the *Big Issue* do so because the magazine's readership is sympathetic to their work. Their ad will have been carefully written, well designed and placed at an appropriate time of year. Long-lasting success at recruiting doesn't happen because we strike it lucky and find a magic method. Achievements are built on a well thought out strategy that reaches out to the right people in the appropriate way. That will usually mean some degree of original thinking and, while other organisation's experiences can provide you with useful food for thought, you still need to work at it and test its appropriateness for you.

This chapter explores ways to help you get out of a recruitment rut. If your recruitment methods are stale or unsuccessful it may be time to take a leap in your imagination, and think about it from a new point of view. Later on we'll look at some specific techniques that you can use to help you think more creatively about the way you find new volunteers.

Four imaginative leaps to enhance recruitment success

Leap 1 – take responsibility for succeeding

With so many organisations chasing volunteers you can easily feel under pressure to find new ways of finding good people. We recently asked participants on a recruitment workshop why it is difficult to find volunteers. They told us:

- 'Nobody wants to volunteer with our client group.'
- 'Our organisation's work isn't as appealing as other charities'.'
- 'People are too selfish to volunteer these days.'
- 'Too many other organisations are chasing too few volunteers.'
- 'People don't have as much time to volunteer as they used to.'
- 'There are less unemployed people available these days.'
- 'People who retire early don't want to volunteer – they want to travel, and do other things.'

While some of the above comments reflect actual social changes (such as a drop in unemployment), others are complete rubbish. What all of these statements have in common is that they are variations on a theme of 'It's not my fault we don't have enough volunteers'. If you take the view that recruiting successfully is outside your control, then you effectively remove yourself from being part of the solution, and that erects a bigger barrier than anything the general public can throw at you.

Fortunately, our workshops are attended by insightful and honest people, and so the above are not the only responses we get. People also tell us that they find recruitment difficult because:

- 'I don't spend enough time on recruitment activities.'
- 'My manager won't let me spend any money on recruitment.'
- 'We don't have a recruitment strategy.'
- 'We don't even have a plan for the volunteer programme.'
- 'We're not very clear on who we're looking for.'
- 'We only offer volunteers boring work to do.'
- 'I can't believe that anybody would want to volunteer with us – even though there's plenty to do!'

These responses acknowledge that success is within our control, if only we take responsibility for overcoming the obstacles we create within ourselves and our organisation. Unquestionably, recruiting volunteers is a challenge made harder by rapidly changing social norms. But those changes also present new possibilities and opportunities.

You can begin to change your viewpoint by conducting an honest evaluation of the barriers you and your organisation put in the way of success. These might include negative beliefs or attitudes towards potential volunteers, an unwillingness to commit enough time or resources to volunteer recruitment and management, or assumptions that your attempts at recruitment will fail before you've even begun. For some organisations, the biggest imaginative leap is to realise that the causes of failure lie within.

Leap 2 – don't be afraid to experiment

One of the reasons that many recruiters would rather follow the herd and copy other organisations' recruitment methods is fear of failure. After all, if we try something new it might not work.

Recently, one of Britain's leading banks ran a major advertising campaign telling us how big they are. A big actor stood on top of a big skyscraper in a big city to tell us that big is best and, as this bank is one of the biggest, then we should trust them with our money. Unfortunately the message that the public read into the ad was that big equals impersonal and bureaucratic. The campaign hit our TV screens around the time that several major banks were closing a lot of branches, and there was public outcry. Just at the point when customers were saying that they wanted local, personal, service this particular bank was perceived to be selling itself on the opposite qualities. The bank's campaign bombed, much to its competitors' delight.

Even multinational corporations get their marketing and advertising strategies wrong. In spite of having departments stuffed with marketing graduates, and being wealthy enough to hire the best and most creative advertising agencies, they still make mistakes. How comforting this is! Accept that if they can get it wrong, so can we. But don't let this put you off.

Your experiments will clearly be limited by your budgets and time. Make sure what you do is in tune with your strategic aims, and the organisation's values. But with these points in mind, and particularly if your old tried and tested methods are no longer working, try something new. Success frequently comes from experimentation and taking risks.

> Kensington and Chelsea Volunteer Bureau, who promote volunteering in their area and find volunteers for all sorts of organisations within their borough, wanted to attract more young professionals to voluntary work. To do this they wanted to get their recruitment message into the kinds of shops and venues that younger people frequent. The bureau director, Jamie Thomas, realised that the usual kinds of recruitment posters were too dry and boring to have any real impact in these places. What was needed was a more glamorous, glossier, approach. Thomas gave a new twist to one of the oldest advertising adages – 'sex sells'. It was a risk. Using seductive images of attractive models, and a clever strapline, he created a poster that fashionable shops were happy to put up because it was in keeping with their image. As a result, the bureau successfully reached young people in a new way. As a spin-off, the campaign created wider press interest in this unusual approach to volunteer recruitment, which further publicised the bureau's message to young professionals.

Some of your experiments will fail. It's a shame when they do, but not a licence to start gnashing your teeth. Every failure has something to teach us, so take time to learn the lessons. It is quite likely you may be able to adapt your experiment and try it again. You can use some of the following questions to help you assess what went wrong:

- Did you focus your recruitment message on a sufficient number of the right people?
- What could have made your audience unreceptive – was it a bad time of year for people to consider volunteering, for instance?
- Was your message understood?
- Were you recruiting at the right location?
- Did you make any wrong assumptions about your audience?
- Were you let down by poor design or presentation?
- Were you in competition with another organisation?
- Were you asking too much of people?
- Did you fail to put yourself in your audience's shoes, or talk too much from your own perspective?
- Did you give up too soon?

Of course, you could be really clever and test your proposed recruitment strategy against some of these questions *before* you implement it. You can then compare your thinking during the planning stage with your actual experience to see what you learn. Some of the above questions may be hard for you to answer. If so, what can you do to find out? Who can you ask? Are there people in your target audience from whom you could get some feedback?

The last of the questions listed above – 'Did you give up too soon?' – is worth particular mention at this point. It is very easy to have high expectations of your recruitment activity, hoping that as soon as people have heard about volunteering with you, they will rush to sign up. If only! People may need to encounter your message several times before they are prompted to respond. Think about how often you see ads for chocolate. Manufacturers work hard to keep the presence of their latest delight in front of us. They don't expect you to become a loyal customer after hearing about it just once. They know you have other choices.

What other choices could your audience be making about their use of time, or the voluntary work they might do? How easily will they be able to find out about you if they decide to volunteer at a later date? Keep your recruitment going until you have enough people – don't stop when you judge people have had enough time to respond.

Be bold. Take risks. Try out new ideas. If they don't work at first, adapt them based on your assessment and feedback. And don't give up too soon.

Leap 3 – network with other organisations

Consider breaking new ground by working with other organisations in your field. Often we see them as competitors – an unfortunate habit we've perhaps picked up from the business world. If, however, we see them as complementing our role (which is invariably the case, as two organisations seldom fulfil exactly the same brief) then it encourages a more cooperative spirit.

Around the country volunteer coordinators are now setting up their own network meetings to share good practice and support each other. Sometimes a council for voluntary service or volunteer bureau hosts this, but we also know of examples where the coordinators themselves have taken the initiative to network. The sharing of ideas and resources not only strengthens individual organisations, but also the sector as a whole. Networks like these disseminate good practice and are an opportunity to hear what others have learned along the way. Why try and undertake a piece of work from scratch – going through the steep learning curve and making mistakes – if someone has already been there before you and can show you the way?

If you are writing, say, a volunteer policy, ask to see what others have done, then blend and adapt them to write your own. And when it comes to recruitment, your network can give you valuable information about trends in your area. If you are finding it hard to recruit, it can be very reassuring to know that others are experiencing a slump as well. The successes and failures of others provide us with useful data to fuel and shape our own creative thinking.

Cooperating with other organisations can also go beyond the sharing of information and good practice. Why not run joint recruitment drives? Take two organisations working in the field of domestic violence. Although they seek to address similar needs, they offer very different services. Both organisations' recruitment message would say similar things about the needs and issues around domestic violence, but they would differ about the range of volunteering opportunities available. There's no real reason why they can't recruit together. Prospective volunteers can then be directed to a particular organisation, depending on the kind of work they want to do.

This approach would work particularly well where publicity about volunteering is also aiming to raise general awareness and build PR around the work of the organisations – this might take the form of a joint press release in the local paper, for example. Two different organisations working together can, in itself, be newsworthy.

Of course there may be times when one organisation wants to address a particular target audience that the other doesn't, in which case they can go it alone. But when there is the specific aim of reaching out to the same audience, it may make sense to work together and share the costs and time input.

Working in cooperation like this will test how well thought out your strategies are – you will need to be able to explain them to another organisation, and expose them to questioning. In working with people outside your own organisation, you are stimulated to learn how others approach recruitment and to break out of old habits. You will meet some fresh minds with which you can brainstorm and generate an even wider range of ideas.

People fear that, through working with other organisations, they risk losing some of their own potential volunteers. Surely it makes more sense to go it alone and try and pinch the volunteers from under their noses? There are two important arguments to consider against this view.

Firstly, as you jointly conduct your recruitment, you are building as much awareness of your own organisation as of your partner's – they're not getting the edge on you, nor you on them, so everyone benefits.

Secondly, joint recruitment also recognises that prospective volunteers have a choice. They are free-thinking people with minds of their own. By openly recruiting alongside others, you are acknowledging this right to choose, and recognising that if the choice people make is right for them, it is probably best for you. The volunteer's choice is important because it takes account of their motivation, interests, and aspirations, and incorporates some assessment of their capabilities. While an individual volunteer's insight on these issues is not infallible, it is a good indicator of where that person might be most successful and most committed.

Networking and joint recruitment will help to keep you advised of trends, get you out of your rut and fixed attitudes, and increase your exposure to volunteers.

Who could you cooperate with in your field of work or geographical area? If you are part of a national organisation that is composed of local branches, why not work with some other branches in your region? Alternatively, if you are a small or informal organisation, who else has similar aims with whom you could team up locally?

Leap 4 – adapt your recruiting to those who are available

So far, our imaginative leaps have focussed on changing your approach to recruitment. This last leap cuts much deeper, challenging the very way you organise voluntary work. Could it be that people won't volunteer with you because they don't like the jobs you are offering?

Adapting the roles you offer

Some organisations are notorious for their 'we've-always-done-it-this-way' mentality. The supposition is that if it worked twenty years ago, it should work today. We've heard so many tales of volunteer coordinators battling the old guard in their organisation, trying to get them to change with the times. As a more diverse mix of people becomes interested in volunteering, the roles that are available need to diversify too.

Younger people, for example, don't necessarily want to do the same things as older people. Gareth Jenkins, formerly of the National Federation of Youth Action Agencies, has been supporting younger people in volunteering for 15 years.

'Organisations are often keen to have younger people volunteering with them, but don't believe that young people are interested. One reason for this is that managers rarely think through the work from the young person's perspective. I've heard countless young people say that when they turn up to volunteer all they are asked to do is undertake menial, undemanding and often dull tasks. The older staff and volunteers only see them as some free muscle, and keep all the interesting work for themselves. In these situations the young people soon leave, which fuels the older ones' belief that young people aren't committed or reliable. In fact, young people are more than willing to commit to voluntary work but you have to offer them the right roles, and certainly not just the dross.'

Jenkins puts the success of Youth Action Agencies down to the way they involve young people in creating the right roles for themselves, which gives them some sense of ownership in their work. 'Young people devise, manage and review their volunteering tasks', he says. 'Introducing more of that methodology into mainstream volunteering will make voluntary work a far more attractive option for young people.'

Every volunteer, of any age, wants a role that is going to be satisfying and rewarding to undertake. Perhaps part of your recruitment strategy could involve a review of the way roles are designed to make them more appealing to the types of people you want to attract.

> When Frank moved to a new town he discovered that there was an amateur dramatic society not far from where he lived. He'd been successful in drama at school, having been cast in lead roles in a number of productions. Joining the local society seemed like a good way of building on this experience and continuing his involvement in acting. He made an appointment with the management committee to arrange an audition, which he passed. They told him they would be pleased to have him in the company. And then the chair asked, 'Is there anything else you can do? We can't cast everyone in every production so lots of us double up as stage hands, staffing front of house or building scenery. Would you be happy to get involved in other ways?'
>
> 'Sure,' said Frank. 'Why not?'
>
> 'Good. Well why don't you pop down to the green room for a drink. Some of our other members are down there. Talk to them and find out where they need help.'
>
> Frank introduced himself in the bar, and told the other members that he'd passed the audition but wanted to hear about other ways of getting involved. 'You'll need to,' said the barman. 'You'll never get a part. The committee cast themselves in all the roles and the rest of us hang about hoping for a spare walk-on part. I passed my audition three years ago and I've been behind the bar ever since.'
>
> 'Same with me,' said another. 'I've been here for years as a stage hand and I'm still waiting to be cast. I hope you're the patient sort.'
>
> Frank saw the kind of work he really wanted to do dwindling to a distant hope. He left, and never returned.

Adapting to volunteers' needs

Adapting your voluntary work to make it more rewarding is not the only way you can encourage people to volunteer. There are pockets of available people out there willing to help, provided you are prepared to accommodate their other needs.

A good example of this concerns people who are unemployed. Some volunteer coordinators have real frustrations with this group of people. As one woman said to us, 'The trouble with unemployed people is that as soon as you get them trained and inducted they go and get a job, and you have to start the recruitment process all over again. Obviously, it's good for them if volunteering fills time between jobs, or helps to give them experience which leads to employment. But it's a real pain in the neck for me.'

While not all unemployed volunteers are short term, they do need to be able to leave at short notice if they get a job. Rather than seeing this as a nuisance, why not organise voluntary work in a way that allows tasks to be dropped by one person and picked up by another? If you are offering adequate coordination and support to volunteers this should be relatively easy. It is only when the volunteer programme is already under-resourced that this will be a problem, in which case it's not just recruitment methods that need to change.

Even if unemployment isn't high, there are still plenty of people out there without work. Younger jobless people want voluntary roles that will give them experience they can put on their CV, while older unemployed people have plenty of skills and experience that they want to utilise. By adapting your volunteer roles to meet the needs of jobless volunteers, and organising tasks so that they can be passed on when a volunteer leaves, you can turn unemployed volunteers from being a headache to an asset.

Mark Restall is Information Officer at the National Centre for Volunteering. He believes that there are other groups of people that volunteer recruiters could be better at reaching out to. 'I'd like to see more organisations recruiting asylum seekers and refugees,' he says. 'There are many highly skilled and experienced people who are keen to contribute if only volunteer coordinators would consider them.'

While some refugees and asylum seekers may have limited spoken English, or lack cash to fund their expenses, those who have overcome these hurdles (on their own or with assistance) have found that there is much to be gained from volunteering. It offers the opportunity to learn about work culture in the UK, increases the chances of obtaining paid work, improves confidence, and introduces them to new people and friends.

All volunteers need some level of support from the organisation they work for, and their requirements vary from person to person. If more organisations allocated the necessary resources to managing volunteers, supporting them wouldn't be seen as a drawback but as part of the investment that yields a vaster return in the contribution volunteers make. Once you adopt the attitude that support is necessary, and individual, it's a short step to adapting your voluntary work to the needs of available and willing people – whether they be young, unemployed, disabled, or speak English as a second language. If the money isn't available to resource your volunteer programme, your principal problem is not recruitment. It is fundraising.

Four techniques to kick-start your creative thinking

Creativity isn't always about being imaginative. Sometimes it simply involves taking time to step back and think about a problem or situation in a different way. You may feel tempted to say 'I'm not the creative type,' because you can't draw, or come up with fantastic new ideas at the drop of a hat. But creativity isn't simply about these kinds of abilities.

All of us solve problems in our daily life. Our minds have a terrific capacity to consider a situation and then come up with a way of improving it. Some people actively nurture this aspect of their creativity, doing the daily crossword in the paper or solving other kinds of puzzles. Like any muscle, the brain needs exercise in order to improve. People who can whizz through *The Times* crossword have often been practising for years, getting used to the way that the compiler thinks and sets questions. With increased experience, and the sharper thinking that arises from it, it becomes much easier to solve the puzzle.

And so it is with other forms of creative thinking. It takes practice. Many people who complain they are not creative probably haven't really tried. And although they solve problems in everyday life, they don't always come up with the best solution. There can be several reasons for this:

- They jump to conclusions without assessing all the evidence.
- They make assumptions based on their own limited experience, without input from anywhere else.
- They don't take time to think through the situation systematically.
- They don't consider all the available options, but leapfrog straight to the one that is most familiar.
- They want to get the problem solved quickly so they can move on, and are not interested in the details of the problem itself.

Bookshops are stuffed with material on creative thinking. Some books, like Edward de Bono's *Lateral Thinking* (see *Further Reading*), have become classics. Other, newer publications collect and adapt existing material, and synthesise it for a particular setting (such as business).

We've chosen the four techniques below, not because they are the most dynamic but because we believe they can be used very effectively to help recruiters think afresh about the job they are doing. In one case – brainstorming – we discuss a technique that many people are familiar with, but often fail to utilise properly.

Brainstorming

Brainstorming is a method of harnessing the ideas and collective creativity that exists within your organisation. It works best when presented with a specific and focussed problem, and when good ground rules have been agreed and are strictly adhered to. Often, what people describe as a brainstorming session is little different from a regular meeting. True brainstorming sessions are rich in ideas and short on discussion. The aim is to generate as many ideas as possible, regardless of whether they are good or not. If people feel they can only mention 'worthy' ideas – ones they consider useful or likely to work – then it will inhibit their contribution.

The answer to a problem will often be the ground-breaking or original idea someone had, but thought was too stupid to mention. They couldn't see how it would work. But somebody else might see its possibilities. Alternatively, one person's idea – no matter how bizarre – may prompt the next person's suggestion. While the original idea may not in itself be useful, it can act as a stepping stone to one that is. On other occasions the solution will be simple – so simple that the person with the idea assumed others must have considered it, or tried it out, already.

In Chapter 2 we suggested pulling together a group of imaginative and creative people within your organisation to help you brainstorm some recruitment ideas. This can work particularly well when you try and draw in people from different departments or areas of responsibility. Invite a trustee or two, as well as existing volunteers, and maybe even some service-users. Remind people that successful volunteer recruitment is a matter that affects the whole organisation and be open about wanting to generate new ideas or approaches. We've found that people are often willing to give half an hour to respond to a request for their input. Being asked to do this is a way of being recognised, and can make a novel change from normal work activity while still contributing valuably to the organisation.

To get the most out of a brainstorming session, follow good ground rules that allow everyone to say absolutely whatever they like. Remember that success is measured in the quantity of ideas generated and not by how 'good' they are. Brainstorming sessions often fail to work properly because proper ground rules have not been agreed, or people don't stick to them once they start. In particular, groups often get bogged down in discussing the merits – or otherwise – of a particular idea, rather than concentrating on generating additional ideas. To make sure you get the most out of your brainstorming session we suggest some guidelines.

Getting the most out of brainstorming

- Limit the number of people involved. If there are too many, some individuals may not take responsibility for contributing. Between six and eight people should be enough

- Agree a time limit. You'll sense when the group has peaked in terms of the number of ideas it can generate. You certainly shouldn't need more than 25 minutes. But beware of stopping the session too quickly – sometimes the group is pausing to think and may get a second wind

- Have an individual who takes clear responsibility for facilitating the session and recording ideas onto a flipchart. It may be helpful if the facilitator isn't a contributor but concentrates solely on supporting and encouraging others' input and ensuring the rules are followed. In particular, the facilitator should point out when people are straying from generating ideas to criticising them

- Clearly state the specific problem you want people to think about, and write it up where everyone can see it. Be as focussed as possible. For example, 'In what professions would we find people with the skills to become good committee members?' is a better statement than 'How can we find more people for the committee?'

- Leave the judgement of ideas until after the brainstorming session. You might find it helpful to have a few criteria to help you decide which ideas best solve your problem. If you have developed person specifications for your volunteer roles, you will already be clear on what your criteria are. You can also allow time at the end of the session for people to ask questions about another's idea – this shouldn't take place during the brainstorm itself

- Encourage people to say whatever comes into their head, no matter how bizarre, silly or irrelevant they think it is. Allow people to have fun with ideas and be playful. They may not be allowed to criticise, but they can have a good laugh along the way.

It is also possible to run brainstorming sessions without everyone present in the same room. Pin your problem to a noticeboard or wall which you cover with blank stick-on notes. Invite colleagues to jot down each idea they have over the course of a week or so, using one note per idea. Once you have enough ideas collected, you can move them around into groups or themes, and discard the ones you can't use. If the workers in your organisation are linked to a computer intranet you could also set up a virtual bulletin board there. You might even offer a prize to the person with the most ideas.

The term 'brainstorm' is currently the cause of some controversy within the voluntary sector, due to its medical application. Some feel that because brainstorms are associated with epilepsy, it is better to avoid the term in other contexts. We have chosen to retain the use of the word 'brainstorm' here as this is the designation given widely to the technique in creative thinking literature, and because it is not a technical medical term. While some people choose to use an alternative word, there currently seems to be no consensus of what this should be and we felt it would be confusing to introduce our own in this book. Neither The British Epilepsy Association nor The National Society for Epilepsy oppose the use of the term 'brainstorm' in the context of creative thinking.

Visualisation

A very powerful tool for engaging your imagination is visualisation. Once you have decided to focus your recruitment on a particular group of people, take time to put yourself in their shoes. Where will they be when they read your recruitment message – at home, at work, shopping? Try and imagine yourself as them. Ask yourself the following questions:

- What are they thinking about in that location when they encounter your message?
- What is important to them at that point in time?
- What are the priorities in their life?

Now try and imagine them hearing or reading your recruitment message:

- What would they need to see or hear to engage their attention?
- What would make them interested in volunteering for you?
- What would make it satisfying and rewarding for them?
- What needs do they have that your message will have to address?

You might try and visualise them as people who know little about your organisation:

- What can you tell them about your work or aims?
- Why would they be sympathetic to it?
- How can you explain your volunteers' roles in terms that will make sense to them?

A visualisation exercise like this can really help you to get away from your perspective and see your organisation from the point of view of potential volunteers. At times this technique can throw up some quite startling insights. 'Why would young people want to volunteer with us? It's not fun!' So how can you make volunteering with you more enjoyable, and then present this element of fun in your recruitment materials?

Visualisation guidelines

1 Organise a relaxing environment away from noise and distractions

2 Take some time to relax – sit comfortably, and keep your eyes closed or open as you prefer. Focus on your breathing for a few minutes: each time you inhale imagine you are breathing in clear, sparkling, cleansing energy. Each time you exhale breath out any tiredness, tension or distracting thoughts

3 Tense and relax different muscle groups in your body – face, neck, shoulders, arms, hands, chest, stomach, buttocks, thighs, calves, and feet

4 Imagine a hypothetical situation: visualise a person who is a member of your target audience. What are they wearing? What age are they? What images, words, colours, sounds and feelings come to mind when you think about them? Put yourself into their shoes: what are their interests, commitments, priorities, attitudes and concerns? Where are they when they see or hear your recruitment message? What do you need to tell them to make your recruitment message meaningful to them?

5 After you have spent a few minutes visualising and considering this person, take some time to jot down the thoughts and ideas that came to your mind.

Challenge your assumptions

Organisations collect assumptions like a white shirt collects gravy stains. It is an almost magnetic attraction and, once there, can be very hard to shift. Assumptions come from our previous experiences as well as from our prejudices and opinions. Add those to the collected, shared, experiences of others in the organisation and they can easily be seen as gospel truth. For example:

- 'Young people don't want to volunteer.'
- 'Our voluntary work isn't fashionable.'
- 'Volunteers are unreliable.'
- 'We never get volunteers with the skills we need.'

When you make assumptions like these you lose any incentive to resolve the problem they represent. If 'young people don't want to volunteer' why bother trying to recruit them? And in a flash you crush any chance of creativity.

What assumptions do you, and your organisation, make about successful ways of finding new volunteers? Even when you think you have a good reason for making that assumption, be brave for a moment and play around with it. Try the exercise below.

Challenging your assumptions

1   Write down the assumption you want to challenge, for example:
    'Young people don't want to volunteer with us'

2   Now write down the exact opposite of that assumption:
    'Young people like to volunteer with us'

3   Holding the new assumption in your mind, start to write down reasons to support your new assumption:
    'We are fun to volunteer with'
    'We offer worthwhile experience'
    'We're not afraid to give them responsibility'
    Keep going until you run out of ideas. They don't have to be currently true for your organisation. You are using your imagination to help you overcome the barrier put in the way of your creative thinking by this old assumption

4   Now look at what your answers suggest you could do to overcome the original problem. Consider the following questions:
    What assumptions are you making about the kinds of people who do and don't want to volunteer?
    What do you assume are the types of jobs people do and don't want to volunteer for?
    What assumptions do you make about methods of recruitment that are, and are not, successful?

5   Take a few minutes to reverse the assumptions you listed in answer to question 4. Consider what changes you could make within your volunteer programme, or to the ways you recruit volunteers, to make your new assumptions come true.

Challenging assumptions can bring enormous benefits to your organisation.

When a youth internet project was publicising its new volunteering website for young people, the members started to think about the most suitable newspapers in which to promote it. An obvious choice was the *Guardian*. Many organisations use that paper's volunteer page in recruitment. As a middle-class quality broadsheet, with a left of centre political bias, it has a readership considered to be fairly well informed about social issues. The members of the project realised that a lot of assumptions were being made here, not least of which was that readers of other newspapers would not be interested in volunteering. They decided to challenge that assumption, and to place an ad in the *Sun* – a tabloid that is not renowned for its political correctness, with a working-class readership and with a circulation several times bigger than the *Guardian*. It was an approach to recruitment that was virtually unheard of within the voluntary sector. But for the internet project it worked, and generated a successful number of responses.

Arouse your curiosity

A lot of assumptions arise from a lack of information. Your experience may have informed your assumptions, but it may be incomplete and may have led you to wrong conclusions. The phrase that best embodies the foolishness of assumptions is 'We tried that once, and it didn't work'. This implies that the activity in question was undertaken perfectly, and that those involved had full possession of all the necessary information before completing it. A person who is curious would say something different: 'We tried that once. Why didn't it work?'.

Michael Ray and Rochelle Myers, in their book *Creativity in Business* (see *Further Reading*) say 'Creativity always starts with a question'. Those who are successful in finding solutions and in being imaginative have an innate curiosity. There used to be a button badge that was popular on school blazers in the 1970s. It said, 'If it moves it's biology, if it smells it's chemistry, if it doesn't work it's physics'. If you ever studied physics at school, perhaps you can remember conducting numerous experiments that didn't work, and the teacher then leading discussions on why they failed. The learning often came from asking why the experiment didn't work, because that pointed to a bigger lesson or scientific law. And scientists are very curious people.

Curiosity leads to answers, which in turn solve problems. Many volunteer recruiters fail where they could succeed because they are looking for an easy life. Their lack of interest means they don't research the people they want to target, nor find out about trends within the voluntary sector, or even try to discover what other voluntary organisations have learned about successful recruitment. But if you are curious you will want to find out about these things. You will want to analyse failures – yours and others – to discover what can be learned from them.

No question is too stupid. Often, seeking answers to the most basic questions leads to the biggest discoveries. Newton wondered why the apple fell on his head, and Archimedes contemplated the water slopping out of his bathtub. By being curious about basic everyday occurrences, they pushed back the frontiers of science. All you are trying to do is find a few volunteers, so it wouldn't hurt to be a little curious, would it?

What are the questions you could ask to recruit successfully the volunteers you need? It is much easier to be imaginative and creative when focussing on a very specific problem or issue. By honing in on the details you force yourself to think through your plans and needs thoroughly. A barrier to being creative develops when you either see things only in broad terms, or when your recruitment campaign is trying to achieve too many things at once. This is the source of the plain old 'Volunteers wanted' poster – often the result of someone's half-hearted attempt at recruitment without troubling themselves with any detailed planning.

It is when we begin to engage our minds in seeking solutions that our brain's creative capacity is triggered. When this happens, your organisation's overall recruitment will be made up of many different strands of activity rather than relying on one habitual approach. The only limits to the variations you can use are your time, money – and imagination.

APPENDIX 1

Who can volunteer with you?

There are relatively few restrictions in the UK with regard to who can volunteer for your organisation. For the latest and more detailed information consult the National Centre for Volunteering (see *Useful Addresses*).

Refugees and asylum seekers and family members

All restrictions were lifted during 2001. However, you need to ensure that the activity undertaken by asylum seekers is genuinely voluntary and does not amount to employment. Refugees and asylum seekers may be reimbursed for genuine out of pocket expenses. For further advice consult the Refugee Council, 020 7820 3085, www.refugeecouncil.org.uk.

People claiming Jobseeker's Allowance

Claimants may volunteer provided they are actively seeking work, inform the Job Centre about their volunteering and are able to attend a job interview within 48 hours. There is provision to extend this to a week, but currently no indication of when this will come into force.

People claiming Incapacity Benefit

Since 1998 there has been no limit on the number of hours someone can volunteer; however the local Benefit Agency needs to be informed before voluntary work can be started.

Children and young people

There are no age restrictions on young people or children volunteering, although children under 16 cannot take part in house-to-house fundraising collections without an adult. However, there is a special duty of care towards children and young people and it is important to remember that young people have other demands on their time such as school, homework, sleep, socialising etc. It is common practice to seek parental permission for volunteers under the age of 18. Check with your insurance company to make sure that volunteers under the age of 18 are covered.

Volunteers from outside the UK

There are no restrictions on volunteering for nationals from the EU, Iceland, Norway and Liechtenstein.

Non-EU nationals need to have a work permit to take up paid or unpaid employment. There is a concession to this general rule provided certain conditions are met. For more information contact Home Office Immigration and Nationality Directorate, 020 8649 7878, www.ind.homeoffice.gov.uk.

People with a criminal record

There are two issues to consider here. The first is to decide for which of your voluntary roles *you* feel it is necessary to find out whether potential volunteers have: a) an unspent conviction (for example, roles involving going into people's homes, having access to substantial amounts of money or expensive equipment); b) a spent conviction (for example, roles which involve regular contact with vulnerable people, including people under 18) or c) details of cautions, reprimands or warnings (for roles involving substantial contact with children or vulnerable adults, or being in sole charge of individuals or groups).

The second issue is to determine which type of convictions and circumstances will exclude a potential volunteer from being considered for a specific role in your organisation. The law specifies this to some degree: under the Child Protection Act 1999 and the Criminal Justice and Court Services Act 2000 it is an offence to knowingly offer work (including to volunteers) to anyone who has been convicted of any of the crimes against children listed in the legislation to work with people under 18. If you are a childcare organisation and wish to recruit volunteers for childcare roles you are obliged to check whether prospective volunteers are included on the Child Protection List. Similarly, if you are recruiting volunteers as care workers you are obliged, under the Care Standards Act 2000, to ensure that an individual is not on the Vulnerable Adults List before making the appointment. Other than these requirements, the decision is yours as to the circumstances in which you will take on people with criminal records.

To make this decision safe, as well as non-discriminatory, you need to consider the facts relating to an applicant who has a criminal record and weigh them up against the requirements of the voluntary work. Questions you might consider include:

- How much time has passed since the conviction? How old was the person when the offence was committed?
- How serious was the offence? Is there a pattern of offending behaviour?
- How relevant is the offence to the voluntary work?
- Have the circumstances changed for the applicant?
- What were the circumstances surrounding the offence?
- How does the applicant talk about the offence?
- Is close supervision feasible?

- What are the resources within the organisation to supervise and support the applicant?

For further information refer to the criminal records bureau website – www.crb.gov.uk

APPENDIX 2

Sample EO policy statement for volunteers

- Our organisation welcomes volunteers.
- Volunteers should reflect the diversity of the clients whom we serve and the diversity of the population in the area that we are located.
- A budget is allocated to increase the diversity of volunteers, including a budget to recruit volunteers with special needs.
- We will encourage all volunteers to claim genuine out of pocket expenses.
- A budget is also allocated to pay volunteers' expenses for childcare.
- We recognise that there are a number of groups or people who, despite wanting to volunteer, find themselves facing a number of obstacles to their volunteering. We endeavour to target such groups and find ways to assist them in overcoming these obstacles so that they can be involved (for example, ensuring physical access, payment of childcare, using large print, etc.).
- We shall monitor the profiles of volunteering applications and current volunteers by gender, ethnicity and disability.
- We shall explore barriers for under-represented groups of potential volunteers.
- We will make sure that publicity depicts diverse images and descriptions of volunteers. Where feasible we will translate information into relevant languages.
- We will select volunteers on the basis of a person specification for each role and the volunteer's suitability to undertake it.
- We will involve volunteers in decision making and changes, especially where relevant to them.
- We will attempt to get feedback from volunteers leaving the organisation.
- Volunteers are informed about what to do when they feel they are not being treated equally or fairly, or if they think somebody else is not being treated equally or fairly.
- We are committed to identifying discriminatory behaviour and communication in our organisation, and to raising awareness about it throughout the organisation.
- We will review this policy on an annual basis, including an evaluation of its implementation.

USEFUL ADDRESSES

National Volunteering Agencies

These national organisations can give you information and advice on volunteering issues. They do not directly place volunteers but some can point you to appropriate local or national brokers of volunteering opportunities.

National Association for Voluntary and Community Action

The Tower, 2 Furnival Square, Sheffield S1 4QL
Tel: 0114 278 6636, website: www.navca.org.uk

Can give you details of your local CVS, which acts as a coordinating body for local voluntary action.

National Council for Voluntary Youth Services

3rd Floor, Lancaster House, 33 Islington High Street, London N1 9LH
Tel: 020 7278 1041, e-mail: mail@ncvys.org.uk
website: www.ncvys.org.uk

National organisation bringing together specialist local volunteer organisations. Website contains extensive contact list of national youth agencies, voluntary youth organisations and local youth action.

National Coalition for Black Volunteering

219 John Aird Court, St Mary's Terrace, London W2 1UX
Tel: 0207 723 5328, website: www.coalition2.wordpress.com

Provides information on making volunteering opportunities accessible to black people within all volunteer-involving organisations in the UK.

Student Volunteering England

In 2007 Student Volunteering England merged with Volunteering England. See separate listing.

Volunteer Development Scotland

Jubilee House, Forthside Way, Stirling FK8 1QZ
Tel: 01786 479 593, e-mail: vds@vds.org.uk
website: www.vds.org.uk

Development agency for volunteering in Scotland.

Provides information service and has comprehensive website.

Volunteering England

Society Building, 8 All Saints Street, London N1 9RL

Tel: 020 7713 6161, e-mail: ncvo@ncvo-vol.org.uk
website: www.volunteering.org.uk

National resource agency for England on volunteering.

Website contains useful information, list of publications, a volunteering image bank and links to National Volunteers Managers Forum (NVMF) and to the Institute for Volunteering Research, as well as special websites such as Employee Volunteering (www.employeevolunteering.co.uk) and Diversity (www.diversity challenge.org).

Volunteer Now

129 Ormeau Road, Belfast BT7 1SH
Tel: 028 9023 2020, e-mail: info@volunteernow.co.uk
website: www.volunteernow.co.uk

National resource agency for Northern Ireland on volunteering. Provides information on volunteering.

Wales Council for Voluntary Action

Baltic House, Mount Stuart Square, Cardiff Bay, Cardiff CF10 5FH
Tel: 0800 2888 329, e-mail: help@wcva.org.uk website: www.wcva.org.uk

Campaigns for and represents voluntary organisations and communities in Wales.

Umbrella organisations

Equality and Human Rights Commission

Manchester Arndale House, The Arndale Centre, Manchester M4 3AQ
Tel: 0161 829 8100 (non-helpline calls only),
e-mail: info@equalityhumanrights.com,
London 3 More London, Riverside Tooley Street, London SE1 2RG
Tel: 020 3117 0235 (non-helpline calls only),
e-mail: info@equalityhumanrights.com,
Cardiff 3rd floor, 3 Callaghan Square, Cardiff CF10 5BT
Tel: 02920 447710 (non-helpline calls only),
e-mail: wales@equalityhumanrights.com,
Glasgow The Optima Building, 58 Robertson Street, Glasgow, G2 8DU
Tel: 0141 228 5910 (non-helpline calls only),
e-mail: scotland@equalityhumanrights.com,
Helpline England Tel: 0845 604 6610, Scotland Tel: 0845 604 5510,
Wales Tel: 0845 604 8810, website: www.equalityhumanrights.com

Promotes equal opportunity for all regardless of age, disability, gender, race, religion and belief or sexual orientation.

Council for Ethnic Minority Voluntary Sector Organisations (CEMVO)

Boardman House, 64 Broadway, Stratford, London E15 ING
Tel: 020 8432 0200, e-mail: enquiries@cemvo.org.uk
website: www.cemvo.org.uk and www.cemvoscotland.org.uk

A national organisation that supports ethnic minority voluntary organisations.

Brokers of volunteers and volunteering opportunities

Community Service Volunteers (CSV)

237 Pentonville Road, London N1 9NJ
Tel: 020 7278 6601, website: www.csv.org.uk

CSV creates and brokers volunteering opportunities. They also help charities and community organisations recruiting volunteers by broadcasting appeals on local radio or TV. RSVP, the retired and senior volunteer programme, is a freestanding project within CSV with their own website: www.csv-rsvp.org.uk.

Do-it

1st Floor, 50 Featherstone Street, London EC1Y 8RT
Tel: 020 7250 5700, fax: 020 7250 3695
website: www.do-it.org.uk

Launched in 2001, do-it is the first national internet database of volunteering opportunities from 250 volunteer bureaux and national volunteer involving organisations. You can get your volunteer involving opportunities onto do-it free via a participating volunteer centre. The do-it site has a facility for finding the closest volunteer centre. Only national/regional organisations can post directly onto do-it.

The Experience Corps

4 Goodwins Court, London WC2N 4LL
Tel: 0207 836 6001, e-mail: info@experience-corps.co.uk,
website: www.experiencecorps.co.uk

The Experience Corps is a project funded by the Home Office to encourage people aged between 50 and 65 to offer their skills and experience to benefit others in their local community.

TimeBank

Royal London House, 22–25 Finsbury Square, EC2A 1DX
Tel: 0845 456 1668, website: www.timebank.org.uk

Launched in 2000, TimeBank is a national media campaign raising awareness of the value of giving time and inspiring a new generation of TimeGivers. Details given by potential volunteers via website or phone are passed on to a national network of TimePartners, who are primarily local volunteer bureaux. The TimeBank website is linked to the do-it site.

VInspired

5th floor, Dean Bradley House, 52 Horseferry Road, London SW1P 2AF
Tel: 020 7960 7000, e-mail: info@vinspired.com, website: www.vinspired.com

VInspired works to create easy-to-access volunteering opportunities for 14-25 year olds.

Consortium of Lesbian, Gay, Bisexual and Transgendered Voluntary and Community Organisations

Unit 204, 34 Buckingham Palace Road, London SW1W 0RH
Tel: 020 7064 6500, e-mail: information@lgbtconsortium.org.uk
website: www.lgbtconsortium.org.uk

National organisation which has a service matching organisations to volunteers.

Brokers for professional, managerial and employee volunteering

Business Community Connections

Business Community Connections has been incorporated into Business in the Community. See separate listing.

Business in the Community (BITC)

137 Shepherdess Walk, London N1 7RQ
Tel: 020 7566 8650, e-mail: information@bitc.org.uk
website: www.bitc.org.uk

BITC assists its member companies to make a significant impact in the community through advice, training, consultancy and networks. They broker a variety of employee volunteering opportunities such as team challenges, secondments, individual or team project assignments, and mentoring or board positions.

Media Trust

4th Floor, Block A, Centre House, Wood Lane London W12 7SB
Tel: 020 77871 5600, e-mail: info@mediatrust.org
website: www.mediatrust.org

Helps voluntary organisations across the UK with their communication by encouraging media professionals to volunteer their skills, time and resources. The website contains a range of online guides, a list of introductory surgeries and an application form for voluntary organisations looking for media advice. There is a small charge for matches depending on the size of your organisation.

Mercy Corps

40 Sciennes, Edinburgh, EH9 1NJ, UK
Tel: +44 (0) 131 662 5160
website: www.mercycorps.org.uk

Mercy Corps exists to alleviate suffering, poverty and oppression by helping people build secure, productive and just communities.

ProHelp

137 Shepherdess Walk, London Nl 7RQ
website: www.bitc.org.uk/community/employee_volunteering/prohelp/

ProHelp is a broker of professional services (legal, finances, IT, property, architecture, marketing/PR) offered by 900 firms to locally based voluntary organisations who cannot pay for professional services. Help is not normally given to organisations whose focus is animal welfare, or overseas help, nor to those who apply for assistance with litigation. Firms can contribute towards a single project, or take on a more longer-term strategic role, such as their employees becoming trustees. To participate you will be asked to have a particular project in mind, and to submit an application form. The ProHelp manager for your area will advise on this. The website contains addresses of regional offices and an application form.

REACH

89 Albert Embankment, London SE1 7TP
Tel: 020 7582 6543
website: www.reachskills.org.uk

Provides free service matching voluntary organisations with people with managerial, technical and professional expertise who want to use their skills on a voluntary basis. To register your volunteering opportunity, contact one of their offices in England, Scotland, Northern Ireland and Wales.

Websites and discussion groups

UKVPMs (UK Volunteer Programme Managers)

Website: www.groups.yahoo.com/group/UKVPMs

A lively, friendly and participative networking and communication resource for all Volunteer Programme Managers working in the United Kingdom. To subscribe, simply send an e-mail to UKVPMs-subscribe@yahoogroups.com.

Cyber Volunteer Programme Managers

Website: www.egroups.com/group/cybervpm

The US site after which the UK site was modelled.

Other useful websites

There is an ever-increasing number of internet sites providing volunteering resources. We list a few major ones here.

Energize

Website: www.energizeinc.com

Energize is a US-based international training, consulting and publishing firm headed by Susan Ellis. The website offers a wide range of resources, such as a monthly newsletter with hot topic of the month section, an online library with articles on volunteering and an online bookstore.

www.idealist.org

This US site contains useful information on recruiting and managing volunteers (under resources for organisations).

Sandy Adirondack

Website: www.sandy-a.co.uk

Sandy is the co-author of the *Voluntary Sector Legal Handbook* (see *Bibliography and Further Reading*). Her website contains up-to-date legal information and advice for voluntary sector organisations.

BIBLIOGRAPHY AND FURTHER READING

* Indicates a selection of books available from the Directory of Social Change by mail order from the Publications Department. Telephone 0845 77 77 07 or e-mail publications@dsc.org.uk for a complete catalogue, or visit the DSC website: www.dsc.org.uk.

Editions were correct at the time of going to press but may be subject to change. In 2004 the National Centre of Volunteering changed its name to Volunteering England.

ABC of Cultural Diversity, conference report, National Centre of Volunteering, 2002

Age Discrimination and Volunteering, research bulletin, Institute for Volunteering Research, 2000

* *Age Discrimination (Speed Read)*, Directory of Social Change, 2010

Building Staff/Volunteer Relations, Ivan H. Scheier, Energize, 1993

Business Creativity: A Guide For Managers, Paul Birch and Brian Clegg, Kogan Page, 1995

* *Community Fundraising: the Effective Use of Volunteer Networks*, Harry Brown (ed.), Directory of Social Change, 2002

* *The Complete Volunteer Management Handbook*, Steve McCurley, Rick Lynch and Rob Jackson Directory of Social Change, 3rd edition, 2012

Creativity in Business, Michael Ray and Rochelle Myers, Doubleday, 1989

* *The DIY Guide to Public Relations*, Moi Ali, Directory of Social Change, 2nd edition, 1999

Free for All, a study of free professional help available to voluntary and community organisations, Home Office Active Community Unit, 2001, available on www.homeoffice.gov.uk/comrace/active

'Individualism and New Styles of Youth Volunteering: an Empirical Exploration', Lesley Hustinx in *Voluntary Action*, Vol. 3, No. 2, Spring 2001

'Initial Telephone Contact of Prospective Volunteers with Nonprofits: An Operational Definition of Quality and Norms for 500 Agencies', Charles J. Hobson and Kathryn L. Malec in *The Journal of Volunteer Administration*, Summer/Fall 1999

'Including Members with Disabilities in Your Service Program, Recommendations for Developing a Recruiting and Application Process that is Accessible to Persons with All Types of Disabilities', *Disability Inclusion Resources for AmeriCorps*

Program in Texas, from www.onestarfoundation.org/onestar/americorps/disability/respon.html

* *Keeping Volunteers: A Guide to Retaining Good People*, Steve McCurley and Rick Lynch, Directory of Social Change, 1st edition, 2007

Lateral Thinking, Edward de Bono, Penguin Books, 1970

My Time, My Community, Myself, Experiences of Volunteering within the Black Community, Seema Bhasin, The National Centre of Volunteering, 1997

Potential of a Lifetime, Jane Forster, Research Summary No.s 1 & 2, The Carnegie United Kingdom Trust, 1998

'Recruiting and retaining black volunteers: a study of a black voluntary organisation', Dr Nadia Joanne Britton, in *Voluntary Action*, Vol. 1, No. 3, Autumn 1999

A Route to Opportunity: a series of five booklets about volunteering by young people/black people/older people/unemployed people and people with disabilities, Filiz Niyazi, National Centre of Volunteering, 1996

Recruiting Male Volunteers, A guide based on exploratory research, Stephanie T. Blackman, Corporation for National Service, Washington, 1999, available free of charge from www.energizeinc.com/download/blackman.pdf

Somebody Else's Problem, Working with Black Volunteers, NAVB, 2001

'Student Volunteering, Best Days', Alex Peel in *Volunteering Magazine*, No. 75, Feb 2002

What Young People Want from Volunteering, Katherine Gaskin, Institute for Volunteering Research Bulletin, 1998

The Virtual Volunteering Guidebook, by Susan J. Ellis and Jayne Cravens, Impact Online, 2000, available free of charge at www.energizeinc.com

Voluntary Activity by African-Caribbean and Asian Communities in Luton, Jean Foster and Kurshida Mirza, National Centre for Volunteering, 1997

* *The Russell-Cooke Voluntary Sector Legal Handbook*, James Sinclair Taylor and the Charity Team at Russell-Cooke Solicitors, Directory of Social Change, 3rd edition, 2009

Volunteering Impact Assessment Toolkit 2010, Volunteering England, 2009

'Widening the Volunteer Net' in *Volunteering Magazine*, No 72, October 2001